AWAY AT
CHRISTMAS

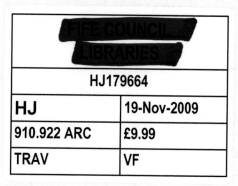

AWAY AT CHRISTMAS

HEROIC TALES OF EXPLORATION FROM 1492 TO THE PRESENT DAY

E&T

First published 2009 by Elliott and Thompson Limited
27 John Street, London WC1N 2BX
www.eandtbooks.com

ISBN: 978-1-9040-2778-2

9 8 7 6 5 4 3 2 1

A CIP catalogue record for this book is available from
the British Library.

Printed in the UK by J F Print

Acknowledgements

MANY PEOPLE have provided me with invaluable help during the research, writing and production of *Away at Christmas*. I am extremely grateful to my old schoolfriend, Michael Hatchard, for introducing me to Lorne Forsyth of Elliott & Thompson, without whose enthusiam *Away at Christmas* would not have been published. My editor at Elliott & Thompson, Mark Searle, has been hugely supportive – while demonstrating commendable tolerance of my many foibles – as has his capable assistant, Ellen Marshall. My agent, Roger Field, has once again exercised great care in proof-reading and editing the manuscript and helping me to avoid the many pitfalls that await authors.

Alasdair Macleod and Jools Cole of The Royal Geographical Society have both been notably generous with their time in assisting me with both research and marketing ideas. In producing such marvellously clear and informative maps and end-papers, the cartographer, John Plumer, has made an enormous contribution. Thanks must also go to Helen Szirtes, Nicky Gyopari and Clive Hebard. My long-suffering wife, Amanda, continues to let me toil away at weekends and in the evenings, always putting food on the table, even though I all too often allow it to go tepid – or even cold. When I first started writing my Christmas booklets – from which this book has grown – our late, dear friend, Trish McGregor, gave me the encouragement that I needed to continue.

Foreword by Sir Ranulph Fiennes

BOTH DURING my Army days, and more recently, while exploring some of the more inhospitable regions on Earth, I have often found myself 'away at Christmas'. It could be a time of lonely reflection: should I not really have been enjoying a traditional family celebration on Exmoor, rather than fighting the elements in the great outdoors?

Away at Christmas comprises varied and fascinating descriptions of Christmases past, as spent by a wide range of explorers, adventurers, sailors, soldiers and travellers. As I can confirm from my own experience, Christmas was seldom – if ever – completely forgotten, however unfavourable the circumstances.

Some of these Christmases are joyous, rather more are distinctly muted while a few are dominated by nothing less than a struggle for survival. However, all are fascinating, particularly with the accounts placed in their proper context.

The sequence of increasingly austere Christmas celebrations of Sir John Ross and his companions during their 'famous sojourn of four winters in the Arctic' illustrates the point. The first year they enjoyed 'an unusually liberal dinner, of which roast beef from our Galloway ox formed the essential and orthodox portion'; four years later 'a fox having been taken, served for our Christmas dinner'.

With long-forgotten expeditions competing for space with well-known tales, the reader also gets a feeling for the long struggle to get to know and understand our planet. All these factors combine to make *Away at Christmas* what it is – a thoroughly entertaining read.

INTRODUCTION

ON 30 OCTOBER 1939 *Life* magazine published an article by Charles J. V. Murray about Rear-Admiral Richard E. Byrd, the first man to fly over both the North and South Poles: 'One of the remarkable facts about Admiral Byrd's success is that it has been accomplished in a dying profession. The professional explorer is an anachronistic fragment, caught, like the kangaroo, behind the evolutionary eight-ball. A romanticist, he is suspect in a materialistic world. Doomed by a shrinking geography to comb comparatively worthless vacancies, he may even be ashamed to justify exploring for exploring's sake.'

In *Little Gidding,* T. S. Eliot takes a rather different view:

> *We shall not cease from exploration*
> *And the end of all our exploring*
> *Will be to arrive where we started*
> *And know the place for the first time.*

Less than three months into his epic three-year, round-the-world voyage, Joshua Slocum (see entry for 1897) described the motivation of many explorers when he wrote: 'I had penetrated a mystery, and, by the way, I had sailed through a fog. I had met Neptune in his wrath, but he found that I had not treated him with contempt, and so he suffered me to go on and explore.'

Of course the nature of exploration has changed with the passage of time. Many of the early explorers would not have thought of themselves as explorers. They were a mixture of opportunists, traders, government servants, pirates or whalers. The Royal Geographical Society now places more

1

emphasis on providing 'a dynamic world centre for geographical learning – supporting research, education, expeditions and fieldwork, as well as promoting public engagement and informed enjoyment of our world', rather than on 'exploring for exploring's sake'.

There are other, compelling, factors at play. On 28 August 2007 it was reported in the *Guardian* that the North West Passage was 'nearly ice-free for the first time since records began'. Climate change – together with its many, yet-to-be-understood, ramifications – has rapidly risen to the top of governments' agendas and explorers have come into their own once again. If, in T. S. Eliot's words, we do not 'know the place for the first time', there may well be no place left to know.

For this book I have researched how adventurers – explorers, travellers and 'free spirits' – have spent Christmas over the past 500 or so years. Unlike my wartime anthology, *Home for Christmas*, much of the material in this book comes from diaries, or narratives written up after the event. There were few opportunities to send letters from such far-flung corners of the earth. While *Away at Christmas* has no pretences as a comprehensive history of exploration, it nevertheless encompasses the spread of European influence (sources and relevance permitting). Concise background information has been included in order that the saga of sequential expeditions – for example, the search for the North West Passage – can more easily be followed.

Whether the ultimate reasons for the exploits described herein were political ambition, personal vanity, territorial expansion, scientific advancement, proselytizing, fortune-seeking or the winning of a 'race', such as those to the South Pole or the Moon, one can only marvel at the achievements of the adventurers, a depressingly large number of whom gave their lives in the process. Equally impressive is the fact that these intrepid adventurers seldom forgot to celebrate Christmas, however precarious their situation. As an aside, the reader will discover that the boundaries of our traditional festive fare are seriously tested by such delicacies as seal liver, stewed cockatoo, fricasseed guillemot, tenderloin of musk-ox, fried rock wallaby, penguin or bear steaks.

CHRISTMAS ISLAND

STRANGE to tell, there are actually two Christmas Islands. One is in the Indian Ocean while the other is part of the Republic of Kiribati, in Micronesia. The only thing they have in common is that each was 'discovered' on Christmas Day.

Christmas Island in the Indian Ocean was discovered by Captain William Mynors of the British East India Company on 25 December 1643. My great-great-uncle, William May, later recorded for posterity: 'This Island, known as Christmas Island, was taken possession of, in the name of Her Most Gracious Majesty Queen Victoria of Great Britain, Ireland, and Empress of India, by Captain William Henry May, commanding Her Britannic Majesty's ship *Impérieuse*, on the 6th day of June 1888.'[1]

The main industry is phosphate extraction and the two major festivals are Christmas and Chinese New Year; only 18 per cent of the population are Christians, compared with twice that percentage of Buddhists. The Japanese occupied Christmas Island between 31 March 1942 and the end of the Second World War. The island has an area of around 50 square miles, of which most was designated a National Park in 1989, while the land rises over 1,000 feet above sea level. The island supports the largest and most varied land-crab community in the world: the human population of just 1,500 is dwarfed by more than 100 million red land crabs – *gecarcoidea natalis* – that take part in an annual mass migration to the sea.

Micronesia's Christmas Island was discovered by Captain James Cook on 24 December 1777. Cook wrote: 'As we kept

---

[1] *The Life of a Sailor* by Admiral of the Fleet Sir William Henry May GCB GCVO

our Christmas here, I called this discovery Christmas Island.'
Geologically, Christmas Island is the world's oldest atoll, some
160 square miles in area, lying just 100 miles north of
the equator. The average height above sea level is just 10
feet although some of the sand hills rise three or four times
as high.

On 17 March 1888 Captain William Wiseman of HMS
Caroline annexed Christmas Island and, in June 1902, the
British Government granted a 99-year lease to Lever Brothers.
Initially 72,863 coconut palms were planted on 1,457 acres. In
1914 Central Pacific Coconut Plantations Limited took over
the lease and, by 1937, some 400 tons of copra were being
harvested annually from around 750,000 coconut palms. The
island was a major staging area during the Second World War:
the airfield and extensive road system date from that period.
Christmas Island, with a population of around 1,800, received
its independence from the United Kingdom in 1979.

~ 1492 ~

As every schoolchild knows from the doggerel, on 3 August 1492 Christopher Columbus set sail on the 'ocean blue' from Palos de la Frontera in Spain with three ships, the *Niña*, the *Pinta* and his flagship, the *Santa María*. The *Santa María* had a complement of 54 men while the smaller two carried just 18 men each. The trip was financed partly by King Ferdinand and Queen Isabella, partly by a syndicate of seven wealthy Genoese merchants living in Seville, and partly by the Pinzón family of Palos, who not only built the ships but also put up one-eighth of the money.

It was a true voyage into the unknown. Columbus was convinced that he had reached the fabled Indies, which is why he called those natives that he met Indians. When he arrived off Cuba, Columbus believed he had found the Japanese mainland. For over a month he cruised the waters off the island of Hispaniola (a corruption of La Isla Española, or 'The Spanish Island', which is now divided into Haiti and the Dominican Republic) encountering, and sometimes befriending, the islanders. On Christmas Eve, on the way to meet a young Taíno chief named Guacanagarí, the *Santa María* stuck fast on a reef off Hispaniola.

Columbus took the difficult – but inevitable – decision to transfer his flag to the *Niña*, leaving behind 39 crewmembers from the *Santa María* to found the first European settlement in the Americas since the Vikings had landed in Newfoundland and Labrador some 500 years earlier. It was called La Navidad, or 'The Nativity', because it was founded on Christmas Day. The reluctant colonisers were left with a year's supply of food, sufficient equipment with which to construct a fort, and specialists that included carpenters, caulkers, physicians, tailors and coopers. When Columbus returned to Hispaniola on his second voyage just 11 months later, he found that Christmas Town had been burned down and all his men were dead.

~ 1607/08 ~

Two English colonies were briefly established on Roanoke Island, off the coast of North Carolina, during the late 1580s. Lack of supplies and the impending war with Spain prompted the evacuation of the first on 18 June 1586, after just a year. Sir Walter Raleigh was the inspiration behind the second settlement, the members of which sailed from Plymouth on 8 May 1587. The following year the dramatic appearance of the Spanish Armada intervened, preventing the despatch of planned reinforcements. By the time a relief expedition finally arrived in August 1590, there were no signs of European life on Roanoke. The mystery of the 'Lost Colony' has never been satisfactorily resolved.

Thus the first English Christmas celebration on the North American mainland to have been documented was that of 1607 at Jamestown, Captain John Smith's fledgling colony in what is now Virginia. Under the auspices of the Virginia Company of London, 105 settlers had sailed from Blackwall in the *Susan Constant*, the *Discovery* and the *Godspeed* on 19 December 1606. Little more than a year later, fewer than 40 people were left alive to observe Christmas with an Anglican church service in their small chapel. The officiating minister was the Reverend Robert Hunt, who survived that first service by just a few days. Captain Smith described the chapel as 'a homely thing like a barne, set upon cratchets, covered with rafts, sedge and earth'.

A year later the colonists were running short of food and Smith set off up the James River with a barge, a boat and 46 men to barter for food with Powhatan, a local chieftain with whom he was on good terms. Of that trip Smith wrote:

The next night being lodged at Kecoughtan sixe or seaven dayes, the extreme wind, raine, frost, and snow caused us to keep Christmasse among the Savages, where we were never more merrie, nor fed on more plentie of good Oysters, Fish, Flesh, Wild-foule, and good Bread, nor never had better fires in England then in the dry warme smokie houses of Kecoughtan.

The following October Smith was injured when a keg of gunpowder exploded and had to return to England for treatment. Although he never went back to Virginia, he continued to promote the interests of the Virginia Company, before making himself unpopular with the controlling shareholders. In April 1614, Smith sailed to Maine and Massachusetts Bay and, with the approval of Prince Charles, named the area New England.[2] Attempting a similar voyage the following year, he was captured by French pirates off the Azores and only managed to escape after weeks of captivity. Smith never returned to America but spent the rest of his life writing about his experiences. He died on 21 June 1631, at the age of 51, and is buried in St. Sepulchre's in the City of London.

[2] From Captain John Smith's *A Description of New England*, published in 1616: 'The most remarqueable parts thus named by the high and mighty Prince Charles, Prince of great Britaine [later Charles I].'

~ 1675 ~

Henry Teonge, born in 1620, originally from Spernall in Warwickshire, was later appointed Rector of Alcester in that county. Possibly because he was in debt and needed to address the situation, he resigned his living and joined the Royal Navy as a Chaplain. At Christmas in 1675, the Reverend Henry Teonge enjoyed a boisterous time in HMS *Assistance*.

Dec. 25, 1675. Crismas day wee keepe thus. At 4 in the morning our trumpeters all doe flatt their trumpetts, and begin at our Captain's cabin, and thence to all the officers' and gentlemen's cabins; playing a levite at each cabine doore, and bidding good morrow, wishing a merry Crismas. After they goe to their station, viz. on the poope, and sound 3 levitts in honour of the morning. At 10 wee goe to prayers and sermon; text, Zacc.ix.9. Our Captaine had all his officers and gentlemen to dinner with him, where wee had excellent good fayre: a rib of beife, plumb-puddings, minct pyes, &c. and plenty of good wines of severall sorts; dranke healths to the King, to our wives and friends, and ended the day with much civill myrth.

Henry Teonge also describes the Twelfth Night celebrations on board ship:

January 6, 1675 [sic]. *Very ruff weather all the last night, and all this day. Wee are now paste Zante: had wee beene there this day, wee had seene a greate solemnity; for this day being 12 day, the Greeke Bishop of Zante doth (as they call it) baptise the sea, with a great deale of ceremony; sprinkling their gallys and fishing-tackle with holy water. But wee had much myrth on*

board, for wee had a greate kake made, in which was put a
beane for the king, a pease for the queen, a cloave for the knave,
a forked stick for the coockold, a ragg for the slutt. The kake was
cut into severall peices in the great cabin, and all put into a
napkin, out of which every on took his peice, as out of a lottery;
then each peice is broaken to see what was in it, which caused
much laughter, to see our leiuetenant prove the coockold, and
more to see us tumble on over the other in the cabin, by reason of
the ruff weather.[3]

~ 1685 ~

William Dampier, who was born in East Coker, Somerset, in
1651, first went to sea at the age of 16. After seeing action in
the Third Anglo-Dutch War in 1673, he became a pirate,
raiding Spanish possessions in South America. Having first
circumnavigated the globe during the 1670s, Dampier was
sailing in the *Cygnet*, appropriately commanded by Captain
Charles Swan, when the crew mutinied and forced the captain
to become a buccaneer. In December 1685 they visited
Valderas, 'a pleasant Valley', near Cape Corrientes on the
Pacific coast of Mexico:

When our Canoas came to this pleasant Valley, they landed 37
men, and marched into the Country seeking for some Houses.
They had not gone past 3 mile before they were attackt by 150

---

[3] Until 1752, in which year Britain changed from the Julian to the Gregorian
calendar and Wednesday 2 September was immediately followed by Thursday
14 September, this date would have been correctly described as 6 January
1675/76. The New Year commenced on 25 March, or Lady Day. However, the
British tax system still uses the Julian calendar; thus the new tax year begins
on 6 April.

Spaniards, Horse and Foot: There was a small thin Wood close by them, into which our men retreated, to secure themselves from the fury of the Horse: Yet the Spaniards rode in among them, and attackt them very furiously, till the Spanish Captain, and 17 more, tumbled dead off their Horses: then the rest retreated being many of them wounded. We lost 4 men, and had 2 desperately wounded. In this action, the Foot, who were armed with Lances and Swords, and were the greatest number, never made any attack; the Horse-men had each a brace of Pistols, and some short Guns. If the Foot had come in, they had certainly destroy'd all our men. When the skirmish was over, our men plac'd the two wounded men on Horses, and came to their Canoas. There they kill'd one of the Horses, and drest it; being afraid to venture into the Savannah to kill a Bullock, of which there was store. When they had eaten and satisfy'd themselves, they returned aboard. The 25th day, being Christmas, we cruised in pretty near the Cape, and sent in three Canoas with the Strikers to get Fish; being desirous to have a Christmas dinner. In the afternoon they returned aboard with 3 great Jew-fish,[4] *which feasted us all: and the next day we sent ashore our Canoas again and got 3 or 4 more.*

~ 1686 ~

On 31 March 1686 the *Cygnet* sailed for the East Indies, with the intention of capturing Manila treasure galleons and raiding

---

[4] William Dampier wrote: 'The jew-fish is a very good fish, and I judge so called by the English because it has scales and fins, therefore a clean fish, according to the Levitical law, and the Jews at Jamaica buy them and eat them very freely. It is a very large fish, shaped much like a cod but a great deal bigger; one will weigh three, or four, or five hundredweight. It has a large head, with great fins and scales, as big as an half-crown, answerable to the bigness of his body. It is very sweet meat, and commonly fat.'

11

Spanish possessions. During the journey food supplies ran short and, at one stage, the crew were plotting to eat the officers. While Captain Swan felt that William Dampier would make a rather poor meal, he felt under threat himself, being extremely corpulent. In the event the crew did not resort to cannibalism and the following Christmas was spent on Mindanao, the second largest and easternmost island in the Philippines:

It was about the 20th day of December when we returned from hunting, and the General designed to go again to another place to hunt for Beef; but he stayed till after Christmas-day, *because some of us designed to go with him; and Captain Swan had desired all his men to be aboard that day, that we might keep it solemnly together: And accordingly he sent aboard a Buffaloe the day before, that we might have a good Dinner. So the 25th day about 10 a clock, Captain Swan came aboard, and all his Men who were ashore: For you must understand that near a third of our men lived constantly ashore, with their Comrades and Pagallies, and some with their Women-servants, whom they hired of their Masters for Concubines. Some of our men also had Houses, which they hired or bought, for Houses are very cheap, for 5 or 6 Dollars. For many of them having more money than they knew what to do with, eased themselves here of the trouble of telling it, spending it very lavishly, their prodigality making the people impose upon them, to the making the rest of us pay the dearer for what we bought, and to the endangering the like impositions upon such* Englishmen *as may come here hereafter. For the Mindanaians knew how to get our Squires Gold from them (for we had no Silver,) and when our men wanted Silver, they would change now and then an Ounce of Gold, and could get no more than 10 or 11 Dollars for a* Mindanao *Ounce, which they would not part with again under 18 Dollars. Yet this, and the great prices they set on their Goods, were not the only way to lessen their stocks; for their Pagallies and Comrades would often be begging somewhat of them, and our men were generous enough, and would bestow half an ounce of Gold at a time, in a Ring for their Pagallies, or in a Silver Wrist-band, or Hoop to come about their Arms, in hopes to get a nights Lodging with them.*

When Dampier eventually returned to England in 1791, he had no money but he did at least have his journals, which were published six years later.

Captain Charles Swan was not so fortunate. Having eventually managed to escape the clutches of the mutineers, but only by surrendering command of the *Cygnet*, he joined the army of the local ruler, Raja Laut. In 1690, while attempting to escape back to England on a Dutch ship, together with £5,000 that he had illegally purloined from the *Cygnet*, he was speared to death in the water by Laut's warriors after they had capsized his canoe.

~ 1699 ~

The publication of his journals brought William Dampier to the attention of the Lords of the Admiralty, who offered him a commission to explore New Holland (later Australia) and New Guinea. Having 'sail'd from the Downs early on Saturday Jan. 14 1698/99, with a fair Wind, in his Majesty's Ship the *Roe-buck*; carrying but 12 guns in this Voyage, and 50 Men and Boys, with 20 Month's Provision', he recorded that:

On the 12th of December, we sailed from Babao, coasting along the Island Timor to the Eastward, towards New Guinea. The

*24th in the Morning we catched a large Shark, which gave all
the Ships Company a plentiful Meal. The 27th we saw the
burning Island, it lies in Latitude 6 deg. 36 min. South; it is
high, and but small. It runs from the Sea a little sloaping
towards the Top; which is divided in the middle into Two Peaks,
between which issued out much Smoak: I have not seen more
from any volcano. I saw no Trees; but the North side appeared
green; and the rest look'd very barren.*[5]

On 21 February 1701, during the return journey, the *Roebuck*
was wrecked on Ascension Island. Back in England, Dampier
was court-martialled, not for the loss of his ship, but for
cruelty, having removed one of his crew, George Fisher, from
the ship and having him jailed in Brazil. Although he was
dismissed from the Royal Navy, Dampier's adventures were far
from over. The War of the Spanish Succession broke out in
1701 and Dampier was given command of the 26-gun *St.
George* and duly completed a second circumnavigation.
During that trip Alexander Selkirk, William Defoe's
inspiration for *Robinson Crusoe*, was a Sailing Master on the
Cinque Ports, which sailed in company with the *St. George*. The
Cinque Ports suffered serious damage rounding Cape Horn
and Selkirk, feeling that the ship was in no condition to
continue the voyage without extensive repairs, refused to sail
in her. As a result he spent four years and four months on Más
a Tierra, in the Juan Fernández island chain, 400 miles off the
coast of Chile. Alexander Selkirk was proved right and the
Cinque Ports later sank, with the loss of most of her crew.
Ironically, the Sailing Master of the *Duke*, the ship that

---

[5] William Dampier would appear to be describing Nila, or Laworkawra, Island
in the Banda Sea, part of Indonesia.

rescued him on 2 February 1709, was none other than
William Dampier, who died in London in 1715, before he
could claim his share of the prize money.

~ 1768 ~

On 26 August 1768 Master James Cook, an experienced,
practical and serious-minded 39-year-old sailor, originally
from the Yorkshire village of Marton-in-Cleveland, set sail
from Portsmouth in the barque HMS *Endeavour*. He had been
commissioned by HM King George III and the Royal Society[6]
to observe the transit of Venus from the island of Tahiti. The
Endeavour was formerly a three-masted Whitby collier, the
Earl of Pembroke, which Cook found and for which the Lords of
the Admiralty paid £2,800 (approximately £300,000 in 2009).
Cook was accompanied on this, his first voyage of discovery in
the South Seas, by 11 scientists, including the astronomer
Charles Green, and the wealthy botanist Joseph Banks, who
reputedly contributed no less than £10,000 to the expedition.
On Christmas Day, as the *Endeavour* was sailing south towards
Tierra del Fuego, Banks wrote in his journal:

*All good Christians that is to say all good hands get abominably
drunk so that at night there was scarce a sober man in the ship,
wind thank god very moderate or the lord knows what would
have become of us.*

[6] The official foundation date of the Royal Society is 28 November 1660 when,
following a lecture by Christopher Wren, the Gresham Professor of
Astronomy, the dozen natural philosophers in attendance decided to found
'a Colledge for the Promoting of Physico-Mathematicall Experimentall
Learning'. In the second Royal Charter of 1663 the Society is referred to as
'The Royal Society of London for Improving Natural Knowledge'.

In his daily log, Cook – evidently unworried – noted, more tersely:

> *Yesterday being Christmas day the people were none of the Soberest.*

~ 1769 ~

After mapping the Bay of Islands, New Zealand, James Cook's *Endeavour* rounded Cape Maria van Diemen, before sailing down the west coast of North Island. That Christmas Joseph Banks wrote a series of ever-shorter entries:

> *24. Land in sight, an Island or rather several small ones most probably 3 Kings, so that it was conjecturd that we had Passd the Cape which had so long troubled us. Calm most of the Day: myself in a boat shooting in which I had good success, killing cheifly several Gannets or Solan Geese so like Europaean ones that they are hardly distinguishable from them. As it was the humour of the ship to keep Christmas in the old fashiond way it was resolvd of them to make a Goose pye for tomorrows dinner.*

> *25. Christmas day: Our Goose pye was eat with great approbation and in the Evening all hands were as Drunk as our forefathers usd to be upon the like occasion.*

> *26. This morn all heads achd with yesterdays debauch.*

Of Joseph Banks, Bill Bryson wrote in his book *A Short History of Nearly Everything* (2003): 'Altogether he brought back thirty thousand plant specimens, including fourteen hundred not seen before – enough to increase by about a quarter the number of known plants in the world.'

~ 1769 ~

After the death of his wife in 1754, after just nine months of marriage, James Bruce of Kinnaird, Stirlingshire, left his father-in-law's wine merchant business and embarked upon a lifetime of travel. Having first studied Arabic, he served as British consul in Algiers for two years before travelling widely in what was then referred to as Barbary and the Levant, now North Africa and the Middle East. In June 1768 he sailed from Sidon to Alexandria: his goal was to find the source of the River Nile. Having landed at Massawa on the shores of the Red Sea, on 19 September 1769, he journeyed inland, spending Christmas at Adowa:

Adowa was not formerly the capital of Tigre, but has accidentally become so upon the accession of this governor, whose property, or paternal estate, lay in and about it. His mansion-house is not distinguished from any of the others in the town, unless by its size; it is situated upon the top of a hill, and resembles a prison rather than a palace; for there are in and about it above three hundred persons in irons, some of whom have been there for twenty years, mostly with a view to extort money from them; and, what is the most unhappy even when they have paid the sum of money which he asks, they do not get their deliverance from his merciless hands; most of them are kept in cages like wild beasts, and treated every way in the same manner. What deservedly interested our travellers most was, the appearance of their kind and hospitable landlord, Janni ...

He conducted them through a court yard planted with

jessamine, to a very neat, and, at the same time, large room, furnished with a silk sofa; the floor was covered with Persian carpets and cushions. All round, flowers and green leaves were strewed upon the outer yard; and the windows and sides of the room stuck full of evergreens, in commemoration of the Christmas festival that was at hand ... Water was immediately procured to wash their feet. And here began another contention, Janni insisted upon doing this himself, which made Mr. Bruce run out into the yard, and declare he would not suffer it. After this, the like dispute took place among the servants. It was always a ceremony in Abyssinia, to wash the feet of those that came from Cairo, and who are understood to have been pilgrims at Jerusalem.

This was no sooner finished, than a great dinner was brought, exceedingly well dressed. But no consideration or intreaty could prevail upon their kind landlord to sit down and partake with them. He would stand all the time, with a clean towel in his hand, though he had plenty of servants; and afterwards dined with some visitors, who had come out of curiosity, to see a man arrived from so far.

Having reached Gondar, the capital of Abyssinia (now Ethiopia), on 14 February 1770, Bruce then became involved, as a newly recruited member of the ruler's household, in the suppression of a rebellion. When that was successfully concluded, the only reward sought by Bruce was that he should be permitted, by royal prerogative, to seek the source of the Nile. This request was granted and, on 3 November 1770, he discovered the source of the Blue Nile, at Lake Tana in the Ethiopian Highlands.[7] Unfortunately, when Bruce

---

[7] The White Nile, which has its origins in the headwaters of Lake Victoria, meets the waters of the Blue Nile at Khartoum.

returned to London in 1774, after 12 years of ground-breaking travel, his stories were widely considered to be too fabulous to be credible.[8] Following a period of 'short-lived triumph', he married for a second time and retired to his estates to nurse his wounds in private. It was only after the death of his wife in 1785 that Bruce began to write up his travels, which were published in five octavo volumes in 1790. Having struck his head in falling down a staircase at Kinnaird after a dinner party, he died on 27 April 1794, at the age of 63.

~ 1770 ~

Having successfully mapped the coast of New Zealand, with only a few minor errors, James Cook sailed west, first reaching the Australian coastline on 19 April 1770. Nine days later the *Endeavour* made landfall at a place that they named Botany Bay on account of the numerous botanical specimens collected there.[9] On 10 June 1770 the *Endeavour* stuck fast on rocks off the Great Barrier Reef and emergency repairs meant that it wasn't until 9 October that they reached Batavia in the Dutch East Indies (now Jakarta in the Republic of Indonesia). It then took two-and-a-half months to refit the ship prior to the voyage home. Leaving the bodies of eight of his crew in the local cemetery, Cook had intended to depart on Christmas Day. His preoccupation with the frantic

---

[8] An example was his description of a royal wedding feast, during which strips of meat really were sliced from living beasts.

[9] On 29 April 1770 Joseph Banks wrote: 'No signs of people were to be seen; in the house in which the children were yesterday was left every individual thing which we had thrown to them; Dr. Solander and myself went a little way into the woods and found many plants, but saw nothing like people.'

preparations for their departure, coupled with a last-minute altercation with their Dutch hosts, put all thoughts of Christmas out of Cook's mind:

Tuesday, 25th. Having now compleatly refitted the ship, and taken in a sufficient quantity of Provisions of all kinds, I this afternoon took leave of the General, and such others of the principal Gentlemen as I had any connection with, all of whom upon every occasion gave me all the assistance I required. A small dispute, however, now hapned between me and some of the Dutch Naval Officers about a Seaman that had run from one of the Dutch Ships in the Road, and enter'd on board mine; this man the General demanded as a Subject of Holland, and I promised to deliver him up provided he was not an English Subject, and sent the necessary orders on board for that purpose. In the morning the Commodore's Captain came and told me that he had been on board my ship for the man, but that the Officer had refused to give him up, alledging that he was an Englishman, and that he, the Captain, was just then come from the General to demand the man of me as a Deanish Subject, he standing upon their Ship's books. I told him that I believed there must be some mistake in the General's message, for I apprehended he would not demand a Deanish Seaman from me who had committed no other crime than preferring the English Service before that of the Dutch; but to convince him how unwilling I was to disoblige any one concerned, I had sent orders on board to deliver the man to him in case he was found to be a Foreigner; but as that was not done I suspected that the man was a Subject of England, and if I found him to be such I was resolved to keep him. Soon after this I received a letter from Mr. Hicks, which I

carried to the Shabander[10] and desired that it might be shewn
to the General, and at the same time to acquaint him that,
after my having such unanswerable proof of the man's being
an English Subject, as was mentioned in that letter, it was
impossible for me to deliver him up. After this I heard no more
about it.

Sailing via the Cape of Good Hope and the island of St.
Helena, the *Endeavour* reached the Downs, off Deal, on 13
July 1771. Cook was presented to HM King George III and
promoted from Master to Commander.

~ 1770s ~

George Cartwright was born at Marham, Yorkshire on
12 February 1739 and commissioned as ensign in the 39th
Regiment of Foot on 19 June 1755. Returning to England as a
captain after fighting in the Seven Years' War, he went on half-
pay on 21 March 1765 and, on hearing that 'bears and deer
were plentiful there', accompanied his brother John, First
Lieutenant of HMS *Guernsey*, to Newfoundland in 1766. In
the spring of 1768 he returned to Newfoundland under his
brother's command on an expedition despatched by the
Governor, Commodore Hugh Palliser, to establish friendly
relationships with the indigenous Beothuk people at Red
Indian Lake.[11] George Cartwright settled at Cape Charles in

---

[10] Shahbandar [sic] – literally 'King of the Haven', or harbour-master, from
the Persian. Among other things, he adjudicated in disputes between ships'
captains and the merchants in any ship of the nation he represented.

[11] Red Indian Lake is in the western interior of the island of Newfoundland:
there were only 400 Beothuks in 1768 and they were reported extinct by 1829.

1770. In *Labrador – Its Discovery, Exploration and Development*, W. G. Gosling describes George Cartwright's experiences:

During the first years of his life on the Labrador he had pleasant neighbours only twelve miles from him at York Fort in Chateau Bay.[12] A small garrison of marines under a few officers was stationed there, with whom he exchanged many visits. On Christmas Eve he gives the following description of the revels, which he said were customary in Newfoundland, having been imported there from Ireland:

At sunset the people ushered in Christmas according to the Newfoundland custom. In the first place they built a prodigious fire in their house; all hands then assembled before the door, and one of them fired a gun loaded with powder only; afterwards each drank a dram of rum, concluding the ceremony with three cheers. These formalities being performed with great solemnity, they returned into their house, got drunk as fast as they could, and spent the whole night in drinking, quarrelling, and fighting. This is an intolerable custom, but as it has prevailed from time immemorial it must be submitted to.

Every Christmas afterwards he has to record the same occurrence, much to his annoyance.

In 1772 Cartwright brought a family of five Inuit to England; among others, they met HM King George III, Joseph Banks and James Boswell. Four died of smallpox on the return journey and Mount Caubvick, the highest peak in Canada, east of the Rockies, was named after Caubvick, who was the sole survivor.

---

[12] Chateau Bay was first charted by James Cook in the autumn of 1763. Fort York was built three years later and abandoned in 1775.

~ 1772 ~

On 13 July 1772 Commander James Cook left Plymouth in HMS *Resolution*, accompanied by Tobias Furneaux in HMS *Adventure*. His mission, once again from the Royal Society, was to find Terra Australis, or 'the unknown land of the south'. In this respect there was a tremendous rivalry between the two great maritime powers of the day, England and France. Having sailed round the Cape of Good Hope, Commander Cook's ships headed for Antarctica. As they penetrated further south, conditions became more testing, as Cook described in his journal on Christmas Day:

> *Gentle gales fair & Clowdy. Therm^r from 31 to 35. About 2 pm being near an Island of Ice which was about 100 feet high and four cables in circuit I sent the Master in the Jolly Boat*[13] *to see if any Fresh Water run from it, he soon returned with an account that their was not one Drop or the least appearance of thaw. From 8 to 12 am Sailed thro' several Floats or fields of loose Ice extending in length SE and NW as far as we could see and about ¼ of a Mile in breadth, at the same time we had several Islands of the same composission* [sic] *in sight. At Noon seeing that the People were inclinable to celebrate Christmas Day in their own way, I brought the Sloops under a very snug sail least I should be surprised with a gale* [of] *wind with a drunken crew, this auction was however unnecessary for the Wind continued to blow in a gentle gale and the Weather such that had it not been for the length of the Day one might have supposed themselves keeping Christmas in the Latitude of 58° North for the air was exceeding sharp and cold.*

---

[13]A jolly boat is a ship's working boat, generally propelled by four or six oars, rather than sails.

The expedition crossed the Antarctic Circle on 17 January 1773, eventually reaching the latitude of 71° 10′ South.

~ 1773 ~

After serving in a privateer[14] in the Seven Years' War, Yves Joseph de Kerguelen de Trémarec was entrusted by King Louis XV of France with the discovery of 'Terra Australis'. Failing to find anything very substantial – and certainly not a 'Great Southern Continent' – he made the mistake of exaggerating the importance of his discoveries, which included Kerguelen Island, when reporting back to Louis XV. He was duly sent straight back to take a closer look. During the second voyage the ships reached Réunion, an island in the Indian Ocean, about 130 miles south-west of Mauritius, on Christmas Day, as de Trémarec recorded:

> *After arriving at the island of Réunion at midday on the 25th, I ordered M. de Rosnevet, commanding the frigate l'Oiseau, to go with M. le Chevalier Ferron, commanding the corvette la Dauphine, to explore a bay that the latter had noticed, and then report back to me at the island of Réunion, where I would await their return. This bay, which M. le Chevalier Ferron had discovered, lay approximately six miles from the island of Réunion, behind a headland that I had named Cap François; at the same time I sent M. le Chevalier Ferron an armed boat, commanded by an officer whom I ordered to assist the frigate's and corvette's landward approach by taking soundings. It was*

---

[14]A privateer was a private warship authorized by a country's government by letters of marque to attack foreign shipping during times of war; the reward was prize money.

fine weather and these arrangements seemed to me the most sensible since my ship, with its greater draught, carried the forges, the nails, the wood for building, and everything that we might need in the case of an accident, while the number of sick seaman prevented me from manoeuvring freely, something that is crucial when coming close inshore.

When, on his return to France, de Trémarec was forced to admit the error of his ways and the fact that France's new territories were perfectly barren, he was thrown into prison. After the French Revolution of 1789, he was seen as a victim of the *ancien régime* and restored to his former position, dying in 1797 as the rear-admiral in command of the port of Brest.

~ 1774 ~

On 22 October 1773 Commander James Cook's two ships were separated by a storm and later failed to make the agreed rendezvous at Queen Charlotte Sound, New Zealand; Cook, in HMS *Resolution*, left on 26 November, four days before Tobias Furneaux arrived in HMS *Adventure*.[15] Cook decided to continue to explore the South Pacific and, between November 1773 and January 1774 crossed and re-crossed the Antarctic Circle a number of times, never once sighting Antarctica, the 'Great Southern Continent' that de Trémarec was also seeking. That year HMS *Resolution* visited many of the South Pacific islands, before returning to New Zealand and

---

[15] Before their departure for England, via Cape Horn, on 22 December 1773, the crew of HMS *Adventure* became embroiled in a dispute with the local Maori people: ten crewmen from one of *Adventure*'s boats were killed, together with two Maoris. HMS *Adventure* returned to England on 14 July 1774.

setting off from there in November on the return journey via Cape Horn. In his journal Cook described a Christmas Day visit from the indigenous people of Tierra del Fuego:

They are a little ugly half starved beardless Race; I saw not a tall person amongst them. They were almost Naked; their cloathing was a Seal skin; some had two or three sew'd together, so as to make a cloak which reach'd to the knee, but the most of them had only one skin hardly large enough to cover their shoulders, and their lower parts were quite naked. The Women, I was told, cover their privities with a flap of Seal skin, but in other respects were cloathed as the Men; they as well as the Children remain'd in the Canoes. I saw two young Children at the breast, as naked as they were born; thus they are inured from their infancy to Cold and hardships. They had with them bows & Arrows & darts, or rather harpoons made of bone and fitted to a staff. I suppose they were intended to kill Seals and fish; they may also kill Whales with them in the same manner as the Esquimaux's do; I know not if they are so fond of train Oyle but they and every thing they have about them smell most intolerable of it. I order'd them some Bisket; but I did not observe that they were so fond of it as I have heard said; they were much better pleas'd when I gave them some Medals, Knives, &c^a. The Women and Children, as I have before observed, remain'd in the Canoes, which were made of Bark, and in each was a fire, over which the poor Creatures huddled themselves; I cannot suppose that they carry a fire in their Canoes for this purpose only, but rather that it may be allways ready to remove a shore wherever they land; for let their method of obtaining fire be what it will, they cannot be allways sure of finding dry fuel that will take fire from a spark. They likewise carry in their Canoes large Seal hides, which I judged was to shelter them when in the Canoes and to serve as covering

to their hutts ashore, and may occasionally serve them for Sails.
They all retir'd before dinner and did not wait to partake of our
Christmas Cheer, indeed I believe no one invited them, and for
good reasons, for their dirty persons and the stench they carried
about them was enough to spoil any mans appetite, and that
would have been a real disappointment, for we had not
experienced such fare for some time, Roast and boiled Geese, Goose
pies &c^a was victuals little known to us, and we had yet some
Madeira Wine left, which was the only Article of our provisions
that was mended by keeping; so that our friends in England did
not perhaps, celebrate Christmas more cheerfully than we did.

On 29 July 1775 HMS *Resolution* returned to England: Cook
was promoted, made a Fellow of the Royal Society and
awarded the Society's Copley Medal for scientific achievement.

~ 1775 ~

The city of San Francisco was founded in 1776 by a body of
settlers brought for the purpose from Sonora under the
leadership of Lieutenant-Colonel Don Juan Bautista de Anza.[16]
There were around 240 settlers, from 40 different families,
whose ancestors had lived in New Spain for more than 250
years, together with 695 horses and mules and 355 head of
cattle. The chaplain of the expedition was Father Pedro Font,
apostolic preacher of the Colegio de la Santa Cruz de

[16] Don Juan Bautista de Anza, who was of Basque extraction, was brought up
on the Sonoran frontier, in north-west Mexico – both his father and
grandfather were killed by the Apache. He was Governor of New Mexico
1777–87 before becoming commander of the Presidio at Tucson. He died on
19 December 1788 during a visit to Arizpe in Mexico and is buried in the
cathedral there.

Querétaro, who accompanied Anza from San Miguel de Horcasitas to San Francisco and back, a journey that took from 29 September 1775 to 1 June 1776. Father Pedro Font kept a diary chronicling their adventures and wrote that Christmas:

> *Dia 25. Con el motivo de que en esta santa noche de Navidad, poco antes de media noche pario una muger de un soldado felizmente un niño, y por estar el dia muy crudo y neblinoso se determino detenernos oy.* [*December 25. For the reason that on this holy night of the Nativity, a little before midnight, the wife of a soldier happily gave birth to a son, and because the day was very raw and foggy, it was decided to remain today.*]

Only one member of the expedition was lost during the arduous journey: a mother who died in childbirth. The party reached Monterey on 10 March 1776, moving to San Francisco that June, where they built the Misiòn de San Francisco de Asís. The success of de Anza's mission effectively doubled the Spanish population of Alta California. When Mexico gained independence from Spain in 1821, following the War of Independence, California became part of the Mexican Empire. On 7 July 1846, at the start of the Mexican American War, Commodore John Drake Sloat raised the American flag over the Customs House in Monterey, thereby laying claim to Alta California, just two years before the onset of the Californian Gold Rush.

~ 1776 ~

On 12 July 1776, Captain James Cook, as he had become, set sail on his third – and last – voyage. This time HMS *Resolution* was accompanied by HMS *Discovery* and the mission was to find the North West Passage by approaching from the Pacific via the Bering Strait.[17] First, however, Captain Cook visited Kerguelen Island, as he described in his journal for December:

Wednesday 25th. At day break in the Morning of the 25th we weighed and with a gentle breeze at west worked into the harbour to within a quarter of a mile of the sandy beach at the head, where we anchored in 8 fathom water, the bottom a fine dark sand … I found the shore in a manner covered with Penguins and other birds and Seals, but these were not numerous, but so fearless that we killed as many as we chose for the sake of their fat or blubber to make Oil for our lamps and other uses …

Friday 27th. The people having worked hard the preceding day and nearly compleated our Water, I gave them this to celibrate Christmas. Many of them went on shore and made excursions in different directions into the Country which they found barren and desolate in the highest degree. In the evening one of them brought me a bottle he had found hanging to a rock on the north side of the harbour, in which was the following inscription written on parchment (viz)

---

[17]Bering Strait was named after Vitus Jonassen Bering, a Danish-born navigator in the service of the Russian Navy, who discovered its existence in 1728. It was hoped that the discovery of a short-cut through the North West Passage between the Atlantic and Pacific would transform trade between Britain, its colonies and trading partners. The North West Passage remained the 'Holy Grail' for explorers for the next two centuries and, as with King Arthur's knights, many were to perish in the search for it.

Ludovico XV galliarum
rege. Et d. de Boynes
regi a Secretis ad res
maritimas annis 1772 et 1773 [18]

This Inscription must have been left here by M de Bougueneuc who landed on this land the 13th of Feb. 1772, the same day that M de Kerguelen discover'd it as appears by a note in the French Chart of the Southern Hemisphere published the following year. After causing the following Inscription to the written on the other side [viz]

Naves Resolution
& Discovery
de Rege Magnæ Britanniæ
Decembris 1776.

I put it again into a bottle together with a Silver 2 penny piece of 1772 covered the mouth of the bottle with a leaden cap and the next morning placed it in a pile of stones erected for the purpose on a little eminence on the north shore of the harbour and near to the place where it was first found, and where it cannot escape the Notice of any European who either chance or disign may bring into this port. Here I display'd the British flag and named the harbour Christmas harbour as we entered it on that festival.

By coincidence, both Yves Joseph de Kerguelen de Trémarec – who never actually landed on the island – and Captain Cook were so unimpressed that they independently hit

---

[18] 'To Louis XV, King of France, and Marquis de Boynes, Secretary of the Marine, in the years 1772 and 1773'.

upon the same name: Desolation Island.[19] However, the French did get there first and so the Kerguelen Islands now comprise one of five districts in the French Southern and Antarctic Lands.

Before attempting the North West Passage, James Cook had to return Omai, a young Tahitian brought to England in 1774 in HMS *Adventure*, to his homeland. Omai, who had been taken under the wing of Joseph Banks and Dr. David Solander, was presented to the King and Queen at Kew three days after his arrival in England, became popular in London society, dined with the Royal Society on no less than ten occasions and was painted by Sir Joshua Reynolds. Within three years of returning to the South Seas and not yet 30, Omai was dead, most probably as a result of a disease picked up in England.

In January 1778 the expedition became the first Europeans to visit the Hawaiian Islands, which Cook named the Sandwich Islands in honour of his patron, John Montagu, 4th Earl of Sandwich, First Lord of the Admiralty.[20] Having successfully mapped the majority of the north-west coastline of America – but been defeated by adverse conditions in the Bering Strait – Cook returned to the Sandwich Islands. After a dispute over the theft of one of his boats, he was killed by natives at Kealakekua Bay in Hawaii on 14 February 1779.

---

[19] To an expert eye, Kerguelen Island was not quite so desolate: when he visited in the *Erebus* in 1839, Joseph Hooker identified 18 flowering plants, 35 mosses and liverworts, 25 lichens and 51 algae.

[20] He is credited with the invention of the ready meal of the same name, driven by his desire to remain at the gambling table without the necessity for a prolonged meal break.

~ 1787 ~

Having explored the eastern coastline of New Holland (as Australia was then known) thoroughly in 1770, naming the eastern seaboard New South Wales and claiming it for HM King George III on 22 August that year, James Cook reported back to the Lords of the Admiralty that it would be suitable for a settlement. Seventeen years later, faced with chronic overcrowding in British prisons, New South Wales was chosen as the site for a new penal colony. On 13 May 1787 the so-called First Fleet, under the command of Captain Arthur Phillip, sailed from Portsmouth: it comprised six convict vessels, three store ships, two Royal Navy escorts, *Sirius* and *Supply*, 756 convicts, and 550 crew, guards, civilian administrators and family members.

By Christmas the First Fleet was little more than three weeks from landfall at Botany Bay. David Collins, Captain of Marines, soon to be judge-advocate of the new colony and who was to found the first settlement in Victoria in 1803 and Hobart Town the following year, wrote of Christmas spent at sea:

> *We complied, as far was in our power, with the good old English custom and partook of a better dinner than usual; but the weather was too rough to permit of much social enjoyment.*

One of his sergeants, James Scott, wrote that he celebrated with 'a pice of pork and apple sauce and pice of beef and plum pudding'. In the event, Botany Bay was deemed unsuitable due to a lack of fresh water and, six days later, the First Fleet moved on to Port Jackson (later renamed Sydney Harbour), landing on 26 January, now celebrated as Australia Day.

In an Eighteenth Century version of the 'Great Game', in which the Great Powers – Britain, France, Holland, Spain, the Ottoman Empire and Russia – competed with one another for territory, power and influence, Jean-François de Galaup, Comte de la Pérouse, had received instructions from Paris to investigate the nascent British colony in New South Wales. Arriving at Botany Bay the day that the First Fleet moved on, John Hunter 'politely told [him] that he could give him any assistance he wanted – except, of course, for food, stores, sails, ammunition or anything else he needed.'[21] After a six-week sojourn, la Pérouse and his two ships, the *Boussole* and the *Astrolabe*, set sail for New Caledonia but neither ship was ever seen again.[22]

~ 1789 ~

While the French Revolution was shaking the foundations of Europe, the survivors of the First Fleet, faced with the challenge of staying alive in New South Wales, decided to 'enlist' the help of the natives. In October 1786 Captain Watkin Tench, an officer of Marines, had volunteered for three years' service with the First Fleet. In his memoirs Tench wrote:

---

[21] *The Fatal Shore* by Robert Hughes, published by Collins Harvill in 1987. John Hunter, after whom both the Hunter River and Hunter Valley are named, was Captain Arthur Phillip's second-in-command and succeeded him as Governor of New South Wales.

[22] New Caledonia, an island in the Coral Sea, was given its name on 4 September 1774 by Captain James Cook, who felt that it resembled the Scottish Highlands. Annexed in the name of Emperor Napoléon III on 24 September 1853, New Caledonia became a destination for thousands of French convicts and remains a Département of France. The remains of La Pérouse's two ships were discovered off the island of Vanikoro in the New Hebrides in 1827.

December, 1789. Intercourse with the natives, for the purpose of knowing whether or not the country possessed any resources, by which life might be prolonged, as well as on other accounts, becoming every day more desirable, the governor resolved to make prisoners of two more of them. Boats properly provided, under the command of lieutenant Bradley of the 'Sirius', were accordingly dispatched on this service; and completely succeeded in trepanning and carrying off, without opposition, two fine young men, who were safely landed among us at Sydney ...

Positive orders were issued by the governor to treat them indulgently, and guard them strictly; notwithstanding which Colbee contrived to effect his escape in about a week, with a small iron ring round his leg. Had those appointed to watch them been a moment later, his companion would have contrived to accompany him. But Baneelon, though haughty, knew how to temporize. He quickly threw off all reserve; and pretended, nay, at particular moments, perhaps felt satisfaction in his new state. Unlike poor Arabanoo, he became at once fond of our viands, and would drink the strongest liquors, not simply without reluctance, but with eager marks of delight and enjoyment. He was the only native we ever knew who immediately shewed a fondness for spirits: Colbee would not at first touch them. Nor was the effect of wine or brandy upon him more perceptible than an equal quantity would have produced upon one of us, although fermented liquor was new to him.

In his eating, he was alike compliant. When a turtle was shown to Arabanoo, he would not allow it to be a fish, and could not be induced to eat of it. Baneelon also denied it to be a fish; but no common councilman in Europe could do more justice than he did to a very fine one, that the 'Supply' had brought from Lord Howe Island, and which was served up at the governor's table on Christmas Day.

Having returned to England in HMS *Gorgon* in July 1792, Captain Tench was soon fighting the French: he was captured when HMS *Alexander* surrendered on 6 November 1793, during the first fleet action of the Napoleonic Wars. Watkin Tench retired as a lieutenant-general in July 1827 and died at Devonport on 7 May 1833, at the age of 74.

~ 1791 ~

Between 1788 and 1868, some 162,000 convicts were sent to Australia, mostly from the British Isles. Many did not survive the rigours of the journey: for example, no less than 277 out of a total of 1,198 convicts embarked by the Second Fleet died during the voyage. Despite new arrivals in June 1790 and October 1791, Britain's new Australian colony struggled to remain viable. Of the fourth Christmas on the Australian mainland, David Collins, judge-advocate, wrote:

> *A further reduction of one pound of flour from the ration took place at the conclusion of December; and from the state of the provision stores, the Governor, on Christmas-day, could only give one pound of flour to each woman in the settlement.*

The men took matters into their own hands: they broke into the stores at Parramatta and purloined 22 gallons of liquor.

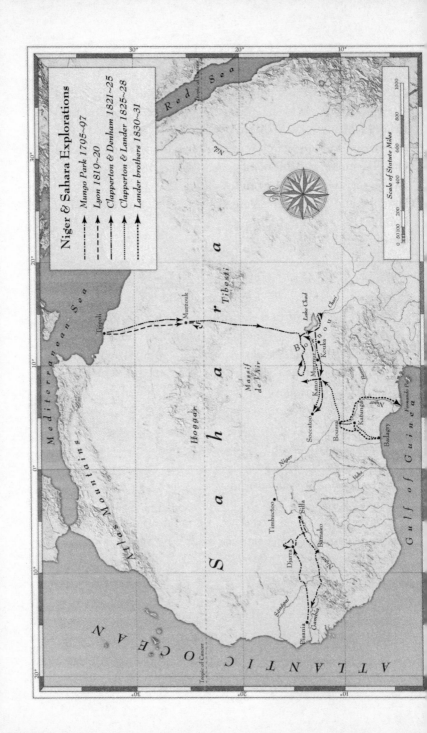

Niger & Sahara Explorations

Mungo Park 1795~97
Lyon 1819~20
Clapperton & Denham 1821~25
Clapperton & Lander 1825~28
Lander brothers 1830~31

~ 1795 ~

In 1794 Mungo Park offered his services to the Africa Association in their search for the course of the River Niger. On 2 December the following year Park, accompanied by two native servants, Johnson and Demba, a free man called Madiboo and three others, left Pisania (now Karantaba, The Gambia), a trading station on the River Gambia. That Christmas they encountered their first major problem:

December 25th. About two o'clock in the morning a number of horsemen came into the town, and having awakened my landlord, talked to him for some time in the Serawoolli tongue; after which they dismounted, and came to the Bentang on which I had made my bed. One of them thinking that I was asleep, attempted to steal the musket that lay by me on the mat; but finding that he could not effect his purpose undiscovered, he desisted; and the strangers sat down by me until daylight. I could now perceive, by the countenance of my interpreter, Johnson, that something very unpleasant was in agitation. I was likewise surprised to see Madiboo and the blacksmith so soon returned. On inquiring the reason, Madiboo informed me that as they were dancing at Dramanet, ten horsemen belonging to Batcheri, king of the country, with his second son at their head, had arrived there, inquiring if the white man had passed; on being told that I was at Joag, they rode off without stopping. While I was listening to this narrative, the ten horsemen mentioned by Madiboo arrived; and coming to the Bentang, dismounted and seated themselves with those who had come before, the whole being about twenty in number, forming a circle round me, and each man holding his musket in his hand ... a short man, loaded with a remarkable number of saphies [prayers or sentences from the

Koran], *opened the business in a very long harangue, informing
me that I had entered the king's town without having first paid
the dues, or giving any present to the king, and that, according to
the laws of the country, my people, cattle, and baggage were
forfeited ... I now took my landlord aside, and giving him a
small present of gunpowder, asked his advice in so critical a
situation. He was decidedly of opinion that I ought not to go to
the king: he was fully convinced, he said, that if the king should
discover any thing valuable in my possession, he would not be
over scrupulous about the means of obtaining it.*

Fortunate to lose no more than 'half my goods' on this
occasion, Mungo Park was later held captive by Ali, a Moorish
chief, for four months. He eventually reached the Niger on 20
July 1796. Despite following the course of the river for some 300
miles, Park was unable to discover its full course and, somewhat
frustrated, arrived back in England on 22 December 1797.

In August 1799 Mungo Park married Alison Anderson and,
temporarily at least, settled down to life as a doctor at Peebles
in Scotland. His account of the expedition proved to be
enormously popular and, in 1803, he was invited to lead a
Government-sponsored expedition to the Niger. With a
captain's commission, he set sail from Portsmouth on 31
January 1805, accompanied by forty-five Europeans,
including his brother-in-law. By August that year three-
quarters of them were dead and Park and the survivors
proceeded down river in a single canoe. Nothing was heard
from them after 19 November 1805.

In fact an ever-dwindling party travelled over 1,000 miles,
under constant threat of attacks from the natives. Although

Richard Lander wasn't able to confirm their fate for almost 25 years, Mungo Park and the three remaining Europeans drowned in Boussa rapids in late 1806, their canoe having become wedged on a rock during yet another native assault. Just one slave survived. In 1827 Mungo Park's second son, Thomas, believing that his father might still be alive – and perhaps being kept captive – landed on the coast, only to die of fever within a few days.

~ 1802 ~

In 1794 Matthew Flinders, Master's Mate, met ship's surgeon George Bass when they sailed together to Port Jackson in HMS *Reliance*. In 1798 they took the sloop *Norfolk*, the first boat to be built in the colony – by convicts on Norfolk Island – around Van Diemen's Land (now Tasmania), thus proving beyond doubt that it was indeed an island. In July 1801 Flinders was given command of HMS *Investigator* and set off on a circumnavigation of Australia, an expedition described 'after Cook's original voyage and the setting up of the colony at Sydney, as the third great event in Australian history'.[23] By late December 1802 they were exploring the newly-named Sir Edward Pellew's Group of islands, in the south-west corner of the Gulf of Carpentaria, off the northern coast of Australia. It is clear from Flinders's account that their scientific researches were deemed far more important than any celebration of Christmas Day.

> *There were traces of Indians on all the islands, both large and small, but the latter are visited only at times; these people seemed to be equally desirous of avoiding communication with*

---

[23] *The Fatal Impact* by Alan Moorehead, published by Hamish Hamilton in 1966.

strangers, as those of Wellesley's Islands, for we saw them only once at a distance, from the ship. Two canoes found on the shore of North Island were formed of slips of bark, like planks, sewed together, the edge of one slip overlaying another, as in our clincher-built boats; their breadth was about two feet, but they were too much broken for the length to be known. I cannot be certain that these canoes were the fabrication of the natives, for there were some things near them which appertained, without doubt, to another people, and their construction was much superior to that on any part of Terra Australis hitherto discovered; but their substance of bark spoke in the affirmative. The same degree of doubt was attached to a small monument found on the same island. Under a shed of bark were set up two cylindrical pieces of stone, about eighteen inches long; which seemed to have been taken from the shore, where they had been made smooth from rolling in the surf, and formed into a shape something like a nine pin. Round each of them were drawn two black circles, one towards each end; and between them were four oval black patches, at equal distances round the stone, made apparently with charcoal. The spaces between the oval marks were covered with white down and feathers, stuck on with the yolk of a turtle's egg, as I judged by the gluten and by the shell lying near the place. Of the intention in setting up these stones under a shed, no person could form a reasonable conjecture; the first idea was, that it had some relation to the dead, and we dug underneath to satisfy our curiosity; but nothing was found.

Matthew Flinders and HMS *Investigator* returned to Sydney in June 1803, only to learn that George Bass was already dead, the ship in which he was sailing having sunk on a voyage from Australia to Chile.

~ 1804 ~

In his inaugural address in Washington on 4 March 1801, Thomas Jefferson, Third President of the United States, said (among many other things): 'Kindly separated by nature and a wide ocean from the exterminating havoc of one quarter of the globe; too high-minded to endure the degradations of the others; possessing a chosen country, with room enough for our descendants to the thousandth and thousandth generation ... with all these blessings, what more is necessary to make us a happy and a prosperous people?' The answer to this rhetorical question was, apparently, yet more room.

On 4 July 1803 the Louisiana Purchase was announced: 820,000 square miles had been acquired from republican France for just US$15 million, or 3 cents an acre. General Horatio Gates wrote to Jefferson: 'Let the land rejoice, for you have bought Louisiana for a song.' Earlier that year Jefferson sought authorisation from Congress to explore westwards, the first such expedition mounted by the US government. The expedition leader was Meriwether Lewis, a former army officer and now Jefferson's personal secretary. Lewis recruited an army colleague, William Clark, to assist him. On 14 May 1804 the expedition – comprising some four dozen intrepid adventurers and known as the Corps of Discovery – set sail 'under a jentle breeze' in a big keelboat from Camp Dubois, at the confluence of the Mississippi and Missouri Rivers, upstream from St. Louis.

Progress up the Missouri River was slow and they covered an average of no more than 15 miles a day, at least partly because they were careful to maintain good relations with the local American Indians. In October they settled down for the winter, building Fort Mandan, close to modern-day Washburn in North Dakota. Of Christmas that year one of the Corps's chroniclers, Sergeant Patrick Gass, wrote:

> *Some snow fell this morning; about 10 it cleared up, and the weather became pleasant. This evening we finished our fortification. Flour, dried apples, pepper and other articles were distributed in the different messes to enable them to celebrate Christmas in a proper and social manner. The morning was ushered in by two discharges of a swivel* [small cannon mounted on a swivel], *and a round of small arms by the whole corps. Captain Clarke then presented to each man a glass of brandy, and we hoisted the American flag in the garrison, and its first waving in Fort Mandan was celebrated with another glass ... The men then cleared out one of the rooms and commenced dancing. At 10 o'clock we had another glass of brandy, and at 1 a gun was fired as a signal for dinner. At half past 2 another gun was fired, as a notice to assemble at the dance, which was continued in a jovial manner till 8 at night; and without the presence of any females, except three squaws, wives to our interpreter, who took no other part than the amusement of looking on. None of the natives came to the garrison this day; the commanding officers having requested they should not, which was strictly attended to.*

~ 1805 ~

On 17 April 1805 the keelboat was sent back to St. Louis with an impressive collection of specimens, maps, papers and despatches while the Corps of Discovery continued its journey in shallow-draught pirogues and dugout canoes. Having hit the navigable limits of the Missouri River, they purchased horses from the Shoshoni Indians, crossed the Continental

Divide and eventually reached the Pacific Ocean that November, having canoed down the Clearwater, Snake and Columbia rivers. On Christmas Day the Corps of Discovery moved into their new camp, Fort Clapsop, on the south side of the Columbia River, near modern-day Astoria, Oregon.[24] That day, Captain William Clark wrote in his journal:

At day light this morning we we[re] awoke by the discharge of the fire arm[s] of all our party & a Selute, Shouts and a Song which the whole party joined in under our windows, after which they retired to their rooms were chearfull all the morning. After brackfast we divided our Tobacco which amounted to 12 carrots one half of which we gave to the men of the party who used tobacco, and to those who doe not use it we make a present of a handkerchief ... all the party Snugly fixed in their huts. I recved a pres[e]nt of Capt. L. of a fleece hosrie Shirt Draws and Socks, a pr. Mockersons of Whitehouse, a Small Indian basket of Gutherich,[25] two Dozen white weazils tails of the Indian woman, & some black root of the Indians before their departure. The day proved Showerey wet and disagreeable.

We would have Spent this day the nativity of Christ in feasting, had we any thing either to raise our Sperits or even gratify our appetites, our Diner concisted of pore Elk, so much

---

[24] Now Fort Clatsop National Memorial Park, Oregon. According to the National Park Service website: 'The sites preserved in these parks allow you to walk where Lewis and Clark and the rest of the Corps of Discovery walked. These sites embody the stories of hardship and danger, of surprising collaboration and adaptations, and of exploration and discovery. Fort Clatsop commemorates the 1805–06 winter encampment of the 33-member Lewis and Clark Expedition.'

[25] Whitehouse and Gutherich or Gutherick were fellow members of the Corps of Discovery.

Spoiled that we eate it thro' mear necessity, Some Spoiled pounded fish and a fiew roots.

On 23 March 1806 the Corps of Discovery embarked on the return journey, finally arriving back in St. Louis on 23 September that year: in two-and-a-half years they had travelled over 8,000 miles, observed and described 178 new plants and 122 species and sub-species of animals, lost just one member of their party and cost the taxpayer a mere US $40,000.[26]

~ 1819 ~

With Napoléon vanquished and Europe at long last enjoying the fruits of peace, John Barrow, Second Secretary to the Admiralty, wrote that 'a portion of our naval force' could not be 'more honourably or more usefully employed than in completing those details of geographical and hydrographical science of which the grand outlines have been boldly and broadly sketched by Cook, Vancouver and Flinders, and others of our countrymen'[27] – in other words, exploring. This senior government servant then set about making it his business over the next 30 years to see that this was exactly what happened.

Expedition after expedition was despatched to try to fill in some of the blank spaces on the world map. In 1805 the government had squandered £60,000 (about £3,500,000 today) – not to mention the lives of 46 Europeans – on Mungo Park's final journey up the River Niger. Barrow believed that there had to be a connection between the Congo and Niger river basins.

[26] On 20 August 1804 Sergeant Charles Floyd died, apparently of acute appendicitis. He is buried at Floyd's Bluff, near Sioux City, Iowa.

[27] *Barrow's Boys* by Fergus Fleming, published by Granta Books in 1998.

On 26 February 1816, Captain James Tuckey left Dartford in HMS *Congo*, tasked with exploring as far up the former river as he could. After sailing some 200 miles up the river and penetrating just a few miles further on foot, yellow fever started to take its toll. The party was decimated: Captain Tuckey died at Moanda on 4 October 1816 while Lieutenant Hawkey, his second-in-command and the last remaining officer, succumbed just two days later. The expedition was another disastrous failure.

Barrow wondered if a small, land-based, trans-Saharan expedition – approaching from the north – might do better.[28] The somewhat unlikely members were to comprise Joseph Ritchie, a surgeon and unpublished poet; John Belford, an English shipwright; M. Dupont, a Parisian gardener, and Lieutenant George Francis Lyon RN. The Pasha of Tripoli recommended that they should join a caravan of the Bey of Fezzan, who traded slaves with Bornou, a Muslim kingdom some 650 miles east of legendary Timbuctoo (at this date no white man had ever penetrated as far inland as Timbuctoo). After a journey of 39 days, they reached Murzouk, where Ritchie died of fever on 20 November 1819. On 14 December 1819, Lyon and Belford set out on a tour of the country south of Murzouk. That Christmas Lyon wrote in his journal:

Dec. 25th. Therm. 9 deg. At 10.45 A.M. we were attended out of the town by the kind natives, who promised to renew their acquaintance with us at Morzouk.

Belford was now much recovered; but I still continued in a very

---

[28] Interestingly, John Barrow never seems to have given serious consideration to the use of land-based expeditions in the Arctic, which ultimately proved to be the right approach.

weak state. Our road lay over the highest and most irregular sand hills I ever saw; the horses with great difficulty ascending without their riders. I was too weak to walk, and was pulled up by Besheer. The hired camel and its load took a most terrific roll, and I greatly feared we should be at a stand: fortunately, however, a man travelling our way came up with us, and helped us to re-load the camel, so that by 11.45 we cleared the hills, and arrived on a heavy sandy plain, over which we toiled until 4, when we arrived at Terboo, the most wretched mud village I had as yet met with. All the men were mere skeletons, and the women equally miserable in appearance; yet they were obliged, poor and wretched as they were, to feed us and our horses without expecting a reward. I bought, however, a quantity of corn, and distributed amongst them; and they declared I was the first person coming from the Sultan, who had not distressed them by taking their small stock of provisions. Nothing could exceed the wretchedness of this place but the water, which was of a much worse quality than any we had tasted, from its close resemblance to sea water. A few old walls of about 12 feet high were in the centre of the huts, and were dignified by the name of the Castle. There are but a few palms here, and the people subsist chiefly by attending camels, sent to feed on the Agool; and for the right to pasture they receive, in return, some very trifling payment in corn or dates. We made this day S. 12 deg. W. 10 miles. As it was Christmas day, Belford and myself drank to the health of our friends in England, in a bumper of coffee.

The pair returned to Murzouk and, not long afterwards, joined a caravan bound for Tripoli, where they arrived on 26 March 1820, exactly a year after their departure.

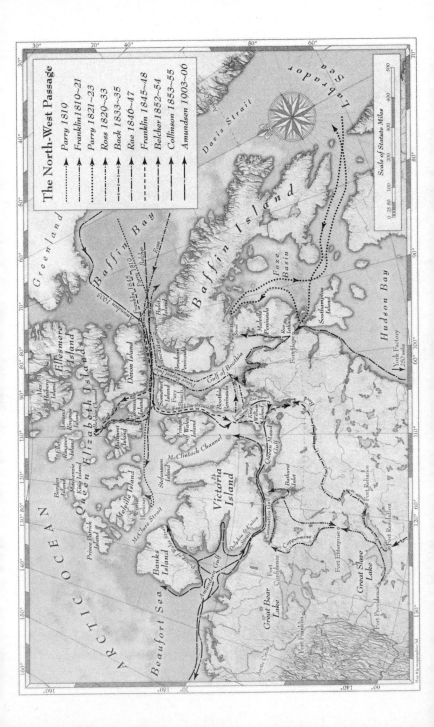

The North-West Passage

·········	Parry 1819
───────	Franklin 1819~21
··········	Parry 1821~23
─·─·─·─	Ross 1829~33
─··─··─	Back 1833~35
─·─·─·─	Rae 1846~47
───────	Franklin 1845~48
───────	Belcher 1852~54
───────	Collinson 1853~55
───────	Amundsen 1903~06

Scale of Statute Miles
0 25 50 100 200 300 400 500

ARCTIC OCEAN

Greenland

Davis Strait

Labrador Sea

Baffin Bay

Baffin Island

Foxe Basin

Hudson Bay

Ellesmere Island

Queen Elizabeth Islands

Axel Heiberg Island

Amund Ringnes Island
Ellef Ringnes Island
King Christian Island

Borden Island
Mackenzie King Island
Prince Patrick Island

Melville Island

Bathurst Island

Cornwallis Island

Devon Island

Somerset Island

Southampton Island

York Factory 250 miles

Fort Hope

Rae Isthmus

Melville Peninsula

Gulf of Boothia

Boothia Peninsula

Prince of Wales Island

King William Island

Rae Strait

Franklin Strait

McClintock Channel

Victoria Island

Stefansson Island

Banks Island

Beaufort Sea

Prince of Wales Strait

McClure Strait

Winter Harbour

Amundsen Gulf

Dolphin & Union Strait

Coronation Gulf

Queen Maud Gulf

Bathurst Inlet

Coppermine

Great Bear Lake

Great Slave Lake

Fort Confidence

Fort Enterprise

Fort Franklin

Fort Reliance

Fort Resolution

Fort Providence

Arctic Circle

Lancaster Sound

Barrow Strait

Peel Sound

Parry 1819

Franklin 1845~1848

Amundsen 1903

Belcher

Ross

~ 1819 ~

Almost 50 years after James Cook's voyages, no more was known concerning the existence – or otherwise – of the fabled North West Passage. John Barrow now made the Passage the principal focus for his explorations while, as an added incentive, graduated prizes were offered by the Board of Longitude: £5,000 for the first ship to reach 110° W; £10,000 for 130° W; £15,000 for 150° W and, finally, £20,000 (about £1,200,000 today) for the first vessel to make a successful passage from the Atlantic to the Pacific.[29] In 1818 Barrow despatched two expeditions to the Arctic: one led by Captain John Ross and the other by Captain David Buchan. Among the 'Official Instructions' given to Ross were the following guidelines:

> *Although the first, and most important, object of this voyage, is the discovery of a passage from Davis' Strait, along the northern coast of America, and through Behring's Strait, into the Pacific; it is hoped, at the same time, that it may likewise be the means of improving the geography and hydrography of the Arctic Regions, of which so little is hitherto known, and contribute to the advancement of science and natural knowledge.*

With the North West Passage apparently in his grasp, Ross thought he saw a mountain range, which he tactfully named the Croker Mountains, after John Wilson Croker, Secretary to the Admiralty, apparently barring his route. Unfortunately, it was simply an optical illusion – caused by refraction – that led

---

[29] The Board of Longitude, whose full title was the Commissioners for the Discovery of the Longitude at Sea, was a British Government body formed in 1714 to solve the critical problem of accurate determination of longitude while at sea.

him to retreat from Lancaster Sound. It was a decision that would haunt him for the rest of his life. Just days after their return, 28-year-old William Parry, Ross's second-in-command, discussed this strange affair with Lord Melville, First Lord of the Admiralty. It was decided to send a second expedition and, to Ross's disgust and Parry's delight, the latter was chosen to lead it.

Parry set about making plans for his follow-up expedition with meticulous attention to detail and, suitably prepared, HMS *Hecla* and HMS *Griper* set sail from Deptford on 11 May 1819. Bolder by far than his erstwhile leader, Parry pushed on where Ross had faltered and, by the time the two ships reached winter quarters on Melville Island on 26 September, they had mapped 1,000 miles of coastline, won a parliamentary prize of £5,000 for crossing the 110th meridian and opened up the prospect of further discoveries in the spring. In his journal William Parry described their Christmas festivities:

Sat. 25. On Christmas-day the weather was raw and cold, with a considerable snow-drift, though the wind was only moderate from the N.W.; but the snow which falls during the severe winter of this climate is composed of spiculæ so extremely minute, that it requires very little wind to raise and carry it along. To mark the day in the best manner which circumstances would permit, divine service was performed on board the ships; and I directed a small increase in the men's usual proportion of fresh meat as a Christmas-dinner, as well as an additional allowance of grog, to drink the health of their friends in England. The officers also met at a social and friendly dinner, and the day passed with much of the same kind of festivity by which it is usually distinguished at home; and, to the credit of the men be it spoken, without any of that disorder by which it is too often observed by seamen. A piece of English roast-beef, which formed part of the officers' dinner, had been on board since the preceding May, and preserved without salt during that period, merely by the antiseptic properties of a cold atmosphere.

It wasn't until the last day of July that the *Hecla* and the *Griper* were able to sail from Winter Harbour, the first ship-borne party to over-winter in the Arctic. The next three weeks were spent probing the ice in a fruitless search for possible openings until, with it rapidly becoming clear that winter was approaching, Parry sailed for home. Unlike John Ross – and despite the lack of any notable breakthrough beyond the over-wintering – Parry was welcomed in London as a conquering hero. Less than two months later he was preparing to lead a second expedition.

~ 1819 ~

John Franklin's enthusiasm for exploration may have been kindled when – as a 15-year-old – he sailed with his uncle, Matthew Flinders, in HMS *Investigator* 1801–03. He had already seen action at the Battle of Copenhagen and was signal midshipman in HMS *Bellerophon*, the most heavily engaged British ship at the Battle of Trafalgar. It was in 1818 that Lieutenant John Franklin first went to the Arctic, as second-in-command of Captain David Buchan's expedition to the North Pole. Defeated by atrocious weather, the expedition was a conspicuous failure. The following year Franklin was nevertheless entrusted with his own expedition, with the goal of exploring the northern coastline of Canada. It was hoped that he might also link up with William Parry's party and they could then explore together to the west.

Sailing 12 days after Parry, they reached York Factory, the main port on the south-west corner of Hudson Bay on 28 August 1819. Two months later the expedition arrived at Cumberland House, a depot on the Saskatchewan River that was 'little more than a log cabin, with reindeer parchment stretched across the windows in place of glass'.[30] Appalling weather detained them there for the next three months. Captain John Franklin wrote of Christmas that year:

After the 20th of December the weather became cold, the thermometer constantly below zero. Christmas-day was particularly stormy; but the gale did not prevent the full enjoyment of the festivities which are annually given at Cumberland House on this day. All the men, who had been despatched to different parts in search of provisions or furs, returned to the fort on the occasion, and were regaled with a substantial dinner and a dance in the evening.

~ 1820 ~

On 8 January 1820 John Franklin, George Back and John Hepburn embarked on an 850-mile overland journey, north through the pine forests of Canada's North West Territories, finally reaching Fort Chipewyan on 26 March. Attempts to obtain supplies and recruit suitable Canadian 'voyageurs' for the next stage of the journey, towards the Coppermine River, met with only modest success.[31] Having eventually recruited 16 less-than-satisfactory voyageurs, Franklin left Fort

---

[30] *Barrow's Boys* by Fergus Fleming – ibid.

[31] Voyageurs were the backbone of the fur industry: they hunted and trapped valuable fur-bearing animals in that inhospitable landscape.

Chipewyan on 18 July. Ten days later at Fort Providence, on the north shore of Great Slave Lake, he met Akaitcho, a Coppermine Indian leader, whose party of 40 Indians would forage for provisions and help them survive the hostile environment for which they were bound. Fort Enterprise was built as winter quarters: the four officers shared a five-room log cabin, the voyageurs had a rather smaller one while the Indians managed as best they could. Franklin wrote:

January 1, 1821. – This morning our men assembled, and greeted us with the customary salutation on the commencement of the new year. That they might enjoy a holyday, they had yesterday collected double the usual quantity of fire-wood, and we anxiously expected the return of the men from Fort Providence, with some additions to their comforts. We had stronger hope of their arrival before the evening, as we knew that every voyager uses his utmost endeavour to reach a post upon, or previous to, the jour de l'an, *that he may partake of the wonted festivities. It forms, as Christmas is said to have done among our forefathers, the theme of their conversation for months before and after the period of its arrival. On the present occasion we could only treat them with a little flour and fat; these were both considered as great luxuries, but still the feast was defective from want of rum, although we promised them a little when it should arrive.*

In such circumstances, they passed a 'winter of discontent' before heading north on 4 June 1821. By 18 July they had crossed into Eskimo territory, at which point Akaitcho and his Indians left for home. During the following 12 months the party was beset by a desperate lack of provisions, by disease exacerbated by exhaustion, by adverse weather conditions, by internal divisions and, worst of all, by well-founded suspicions of murder and cannibalism. The voyageurs were quite right to be nervous about joining an expedition that turned out to be a disastrous failure: just 11 of the party of 20 survived and only a very modest portion of the coastline had been successfully mapped. Having written in his journal that 'we drank tea and ate some of our shoes for supper', Franklin was known thereafter in informed circles as 'the man who ate his boots'.

~ 1820 ~

On 12 August 1819 the 87-foot, 238-ton whaler *Essex* left Nantucket, Massachusetts on a two-and-a-half year voyage to the whaling grounds of the South Pacific. The captain was 29-year-old George Pollard and the first mate was 23-year-old Owen Chase. The youngest member of the crew was the cabin boy, Thomas Nickerson, who was just 15 years old. The voyage was largely uneventful – and successful – until 16 November 1820, when Owen Chase's whaleboat, one of four carried by the *Essex*, was wrecked by the tail fluke of a sperm whale. Four days later the remaining three whaleboats set off in pursuit of a promising catch. Once again, Chase's whaleboat was holed and he returned to the *Essex* to effect repairs. It may have been hammering on the hull by the shipwrights that then attracted the unwelcome attentions of a whale estimated at more than 85 feet in length. In an unprecedented attack, the whale holed the *Essex* below the waterline, causing the whaler to capsize ten minutes later. After righting the ship by severing the masts, they salvaged a bare minimum of supplies and 20 men before setting sail in three open boats for the coast of South America, a voyage that they expected to take some 56 days. On 20 December they made landfall on a small, rocky, uninhabited outcrop, now known as Henderson Island. That Christmas, Chase wrote:

We procured our water daily, when the tide would leave the shore: but on the evening of the twenty-fifth, found that a fruitless search for nourishment had not repaid us for the labours of a whole day. There was no one thing on the island upon which we could in the least degree rely, except the peppergrass, and of that the supply was precarious, and not much relished without some other food. Our situation here, therefore, now became worse than it would have been in our boats on the ocean; because, in the latter case, we should still be making some progress towards the land, while our provisions lasted, and the chance of falling in with some vessel be considerably increased. It was certain that we ought not to remain here unless upon the strongest assurances in our own minds, of sufficient sustenance, & that, too, in regular supplies, that might be depended upon. After much conversation amongst us on this subject, and again examining our navigators, it was finally concluded to set sail for Easter Island, which we found to be E.SE. from us in latitude 27° 9' S. longitude 109° 35' W. All we knew of this island was, that it existed as laid down in the books; but of its extent, productions, or inhabitants, if any, we were entirely ignorant; at any rate, it was nearer by eight hundred and fifty miles to the coast, & could not be worse in its productions than the one we were about leaving.

While three of the men elected to take their chances by remaining on the island, the other 17 sailed south on Boxing Day. Matthew Joy, who was in charge of one of the boats, was the first to die, on 10 January. The following day Owen

Chase's boat lost contact with the other two boats. Pollard described what happened on his boat:

In the course of a few days our provisions were consumed. Two men died; we had no other alternative than to live upon their remains. These we roasted to dryness by means of fires kindled on the ballast-sand at the bottom of the boats. When this supply was spent, what could we do? We looked at each other with horrid thoughts in our minds, but we held out tongues. I am sure that we loved one another as brothers all the time; yet our looks told plainly what must be done. We cast lots, and the fatal one fell on my poor cabin-boy. I started forward instantly, and cried out, "My lad, my lad, if you don't like your lot, I'll shoot the first man that touches you." The poor emaciated boy hesitated a moment or two; then, quietly laying his head upon the gunnel of the boat, he said, "I like it as well as any other." He was soon despatched, and nothing of him left.

It was Pollard's 17-year-old cousin, Owen Coffin, who was 'despatched'. On 23 February the whaler *Dauphin* picked up Pollard and the only other survivor from his boat, Charles Ramsdell, after 95 days at sea. One of the boats was never seen again while Chase and two survivors had been rescued five days earlier, after travelling around 3,500 miles. The three crewmembers who had wisely chosen to remain on Henderson Island were finally rescued on 5 April 1821.

George Pollard spent the last 45 years of his life as nightwatchman at Nantucket. Owen Chase's narrative eventually passed, via his nephew, into the hands of Herman Melville, who later used it as the basis for *Moby Dick*.

~ 1821 ~

For his second Arctic expedition William Parry was given command of 375-ton HMS *Fury* while George Lyon, lately returned from Africa, took command of her sister ship, HMS *Hecla*. This time, instead of approaching the North West Passage by Lancaster Sound, Perry was to go south of Baffin Island, seeking a route through from the north of Hudson Bay. After a difficult approach, during which they covered just 60 miles in 19 days, the two ships edged slowly northwards, before establishing themselves at Winter Island off Lyon Inlet on the coast of North America. Christmas was spent in a now-familiar manner.

On the evening of the 24th, being Christmas-eve, the ships' companies were amused by the officers performing the two farces of "A Roland for an Oliver," and "the Mayor of Garratt."[32] On Christmas-day divine service on board the Fury was attended by the officers and crews of both ships. A certain increase was also made in the allowance of provisions, to enable the people to partake of Christmas festivities to the utmost extent which our situation and means would allow; and the day was marked by the most cheerful hilarity, accompanied by the utmost regularity and good order. Among the luxuries which our Christmas dinner afforded was that of a joint of English roast beef, of which a few quarters had been preserved for such occasions, by rubbing the outside with salt, and hanging it on deck covered with canvas. The low latitude in which our last summer's

---

[32] *The Mayor of Garratt* by Samuel Foote satirises the 'elections' that took place between 1747 and 1826 on the green outside the Leather Bottle public house, Garratt Lane, Wandsworth, London, at the same time as General Elections.

navigation was performed would have rendered its preservation doubtful without the salt.

That winter they established contact with the Eskimos, learned to build igloos, practised dog sledging and explored the coastline. The following summer the ships moved up to newly named Fury and Hecla Strait but the ice refused to open for them. After another winter in the far north, the death of the master of the *Hecla* from scurvy, and the sickening of other crewmembers, convinced Parry to beat a hasty retreat. The two ships reached Lerwick, in the Shetland Islands, on 10 October 1823.

Undeterred by a second failure, Parry soon embarked on yet another attempt. Ross, always keen to score points off his old adversary, described it thus: 'Parry, in his third voyage, penetrated down Prince Regent's inlet as far as latitude 72° 30′ in longitude 91° W. In this voyage the *Fury* was lost, and he, in consequence, returned unsuccessful.' Ironically – as the reader will discover – John Ross, among many other Arctic explorers, later had good cause to be grateful for Parry's decision to abandon the *Fury*, having first taken care to offload her bounteous stores on what was now known as Fury Beach.

William Parry still had one more expedition in him: in 1827, at John Barrow's instigation, he made an overland attempt on the North Pole itself, with the intention of using reindeer to haul his boats, with wheels specially fitted, across the ice. A trial run on an ice floe off Spitsbergen soon confirmed that the concept was fundamentally flawed – and it was back to manpower. Each man had to haul the equivalent of 260 pounds, the weather was appalling and, with the sun never setting, the party found it difficult to keep track of time.

Having discovered that the ice over which they were travelling with so much difficulty was actually drifting southwards, Parry gave up the chase on 26 July 1827. Although they had achieved a 'Farthest North' of 82° 45′ – a record that would stand until 1875 – they were still some 500 miles from the North Pole.

~ 1824 ~

On 5 May 1821 a 360-ton, square-rigged South Seas whaler, the *Tuscan*, under the command of Captain Francis Stavers, weighed anchor at Gravesend, bound for Tahiti. Among her passengers were the Reverend Daniel Tyerman and George Bennet, a two-man deputation of the London Missionary Society, tasked with reporting back to London on the Society's mission stations throughout the world. Having spent three years visiting the Pacific islands, the deputation sailed from Tahiti in the *Endeavour*, bound for Port Jackson, a 4,000-mile journey that took almost three months. Christmas was spent at Parramatta, then some 15 miles west of Sydney, where Australia's earliest farms were established soon after the arrival of the First Fleet. George Bennet recorded:

Dec. 25. Mr. Tyerman preached in Mr. Hassel's private dwelling, at the Cow-pastures (no place of public worship being within 20 miles), from Luke ii. 10, 11: "Behold, I bring you good tidings of great joy, &c." The want of regular means of grace among our countrymen and their families (colonists as well as convicts) throughout the greatest part of the immense tracts of land in the course of clearance, and where population is rapidly increasing – must be accompanied by evil, daily growing more inveterate and difficult to remedy, even when greater exertions shall be made to maintain and propagate

Christianity among the progeny of those who are in courtesy called Christians, who constitute no small part of the aggregate community here. Scattered, however, among the remote villages and farms, there are numbers of young people who would be glad to hear the gospel, had they the opportunity. We merely state the fact, laying the blame at no man's door. It is, however, deeply to be lamented that Protestant governments take so little care to convey the knowledge of their true religion, wherever they carry their arms, their commerce, or their arts, in colonization. The ambitions and avaricious professors of a corrupt Christianity, and the fanatic followers of the false prophet, have always been wiser, in this respect, than Britons.

Further travels took the deputation to Java, Singapore, Canton, Malacca, Penang, up the Ganges and later overland across southern India to Goa, before returning to Madras. The Reverend Tyerman and Bennet disembarked at Madagascar on 3 July 1828 and, four weeks later, Tyerman died at Antananarivo, the royal city on the central mountainous plateau of Madagascar. Bereft without his travelling companion, Bennet eventually found a passage to England, travelling via Cape Town:

On the 5th of June [1829] we landed at Deal. It would be idle to attempt to describe the mingled sensations with which I once more touched my native soil; gratitude and delight actually oppressed me. We slept at the inn, where, awaking before daylight (though it was near midsummer), a momentary misgiving ran through my breast, and I asked myself, "Is it true that I am in England? And is not this a dream, from which I shall awake in some distant part of the world?" It was no dream; but happy reality; and I could say, after all my wanderings too and fro, and round the globe, "This is my dear, my native land."

Over a period of eight years this unlikely adventurer had travelled over 10,000 miles by land, as well as some 80,000 miles in 51 separate sea journeys, in the process becoming as well travelled as any world citizen, either before, or since. The end of Bennet was altogether more prosaic than that of his travelling companion. On the morning of 13 November 1841, on his way to a meeting of the committee of a poor school in Hackney, he fell down 'in a fit, near the Hackney Road' and was buried at St. Thomas's Square Chapel in Hackney.

~ 1824 ~

Despite the failure of Lieutenant George Lyon's earlier trans-Saharan expedition, Earl Bathurst, the Colonial Secretary, was encouraged by the British Consul at Tripoli to send a second expedition to penetrate to the heart of West Africa. The team comprised Major Dixon Denham, a veteran of the Peninsular and Waterloo campaigns; Lieutenant Hugh Clapperton RN; and Dr. Walter Oudney. They eventually reached Kouka, the capital of Bornou, a Muslim kingdom grown prosperous on slave trading, on 17 February 1823. The following December Lieutenant Clapperton and Dr. Oudney went west, seeking the source of the Niger, while Major Denham set off to the east to explore the shores of Lake Chad. At Murmur on 12 January 1824 Clapperton wrote: 'Thus died, at the age of 32 years, Walter Oudney, M.D., a man of unassuming deportment, pleasing manners, stedfast perseverance, and undaunted enterprise; while his mind was fraught at once with knowledge, virtue and religion.'

Clapperton pressed on to Soccatoo, where he met Mohammed Bello, ruler of the Fulani people and the most powerful person in western Sudan. Prevented by Bello from proceeding towards the Niger, then only 150 miles away, Clapperton reluctantly returned to Kouka, where he met up with Denham. They set off together across the desert on the gruelling return journey to Tripoli. That Christmas Denham wrote:

Dec. 25. On our fourth Christmas Day in Africa, we came in the evening to Temesheen, where, after the rains, a slight sprinkling of wormwood, and a few other wild plants were to be seen, known only to the Arabs, and which is all the produce that the most refreshing showers can draw from this unproductive soil. We had here determined on having our Christmas dinner, and we slaughtered a sheep we had brought with us, for the purpose; but night came on, before we could get up the tents, with a bleak north-wester; and as the day had been a long and fatiguing one, our people were too tired to kill and prepare the feast. My companions, however, were both something better: Hillman had had no ague for two days: and we assembled in my tent, shut up the door, and with, I trust, grateful and hopeful hearts, toasted in brandy punch our dear friends at home, who we consoled ourselves with the idea, were, comparatively, almost within hail.

When he and Clapperton reached Tripoli on 25 January 1825, Denham wrote:

Our long absence from civilized society appears to have an effect on our manner of speaking, of which, though we were unconscious ourselves, occasioned the remarks of our friends:

*even in common conversation, our tone was so loud as almost to
alarm those we addressed; and it was some weeks before we
could moderate our voices so as to bring them in harmony with
the confined space in which we were now exercising them.*

The pair eventually reached England on 1 June 1825,
having first sailed to Leghorn,[33] and then travelled overland
across Europe.

~ 1826 ~

Within three months of returning to England, Hugh
Clapperton was persuaded to lead yet another expedition to
West Africa. Together with Captain Pearce RN, Dr. Morrison
and his loyal servant, Richard Lemon Lander,[34] he sailed on 27
August 1825 in HMS *Brazen*, bound for Badagry on the Bight
of Benin. Before the party had covered 200 miles, both Pearce
and Morrison were dead from malaria, leaving Clapperton,
Lander, two black porters and a merchant called Houtson to
struggle on to Katunga, capital of the Yoruba people. Houtson
then left and, in March, Clapperton and Lander crossed the
Niger at Boussa, where they were shown the scene of Park's
murder and were even offered, for an exorbitant sum, some of
his possessions. In July they reached Kano, from where
Clapperton pushed on alone to Soccatoo, the capital of an

---

[33] Leghorn is now known as Livorno, a port on the western coast of Tuscany.

[34] Richard Lander's father kept the *Fighting Cocks* public house in Truro.
Lander later wrote an epitaph, suitable for many brave explorers: *Like the
characters in Mozart's* Farewell, *they had dropped one by one; and they were buried in
a strange land, far from the graves of their fathers, with scarce a memento to point out
the solitary spot.*

independent Caliphate in what is now northern Nigeria, hoping to obtain the permission of Sultan Mohammed Bello to visit Timbuctoo.[35] Unfortunately he fell ill at Soccatoo, where Richard Lander rejoined his master, with their baggage. Clapperton recorded the events of Christmas Day in his journal, which was published posthumously:

> *Monday 25th – Being Christmas-day I gave my servant Richard one sovereign out of six I have left, as a Christmas gift; for he is well deserving, and has never shown want of courage or enterprise unworthy an Englishman. The Gadado early sent to know how I was, and desired my servant to tell me he had acquainted the sultan with all I had said; and he inquired if my heart was difficult as ever, which is their way of asking if I meant to talk in the same strong language. Pascoe* [or Pasko, Clapperton's African interpreter] *was to-day sent to the house of Ben Hadji Gumso, from that of the Gadado's servant, with all his baggage; whether for the purpose of fishing him or making him say what they want, or to make him a slave, I do not know. He made a fair recantation of his faith to-day before an Imam and the Gadado: the latter told him, when he had done, to go and wash himself from head to foot – that yesterday he was a Kaffir, but now he was friends with the prophet. I had provisions sent as usual in the evening.*

On 13 April 1827 Clapperton died from a combination of malaria and dysentery and was buried at Jungavie, five miles

---

[35] On 13 August 1826 Gordon Laing, an Army officer 'whose military exploits were worse than his poetry', was the first white man to enter Timbuctoo, after a desert journey of 2,650 miles during which many of his party were killed by marauding Tuaregs.

south-east of Soccatoo. Although Richard Lander was eventually permitted to leave Soccatoo with all his late master's papers, his problems were far from over. It took him over six months to reach Badagry on the Bight of Benin. Badagry was a major centre for the slave trade and Lander's outraged reaction to the practice soon led to Badagrian suspicions that there was an unwelcome spy in their midst. At the command of Adele, King of Badagry, he was forced to undergo trial by ordeal. This involved drinking a draught of poisonous sasswood bark, which was almost invariably fatal. However, Lander survived by staggering to his hut and swiftly taking an emetic, at which point his status was transformed. The Badagrians looked after both him and Pasko until both were able to embark in the sloop HMS *Esk*. Having arrived at Portsmouth on 30 April 1828, Lander even managed to persuade the British authorities to send Pasko back home again.

~ 1829 ~

While his erstwhile subordinate, William Parry, and the Arctic 'competition' such as Sir John Franklin, George Beechey, John Richardson and George Back had boldly added to their laurels year by year, John Ross found himself in the wilderness, ostracised by his fellow explorers and deliberately excluded from contention by John Barrow, the man in control. Fortunately for Ross, the Government was rapidly running out of money, particular for projects with a poor return. In 1828 the Board of Longitude was abolished and, with it, went the coveted Polar prizes. Redemption for John Ross then appeared in the form of Felix Booth, the wealthy distiller of *Booth's Gin*, who could thus no longer be accused of profiteering by claiming the prize after investing less than the money on offer. He duly sponsored Ross to the tune of 'the utmost sum' of £10,000, which was inevitably to be something of an under-estimate.

On 6 August 1829 Ross re-entered Lancaster Sound, this time in the *Victory*, a second-hand steamer more used to operating a regular service between Liverpool and the Isle of Man. Four days later, he made a crucial decision and turned south into Prince Regent Inlet. Although, by doing so, the *Victory* was entering an Arctic cul-de-sac, Ross was at least able to access the plentiful beached supplies of William Parry's *Fury*, although the ship herself had by this time slipped beneath the ice. Although Ross didn't know it, the North West Passage was now beyond him and a desperate struggle for survival had begun. On 6 October the *Victory* established winter quarters and Ross wrote of that first Christmas:

(Dec. 25) It was Christmas day. There are few places on the civilized earth in which that day is not, perhaps, the most noted of the year; to all, it is at least a holiday; and there are many to whom it is somewhat more. The elements themselves seemed to have determined that it should be a noted day to us, for it commenced with a most beautiful and splendid aurora, occupying the whole vault above. At first, and for many hours, it displayed a succession of arches, gradually increasing in altitude as they advanced from the east and proceeded towards the western side of the horizon; while the succession of changes was not less brilliant than any that we had formerly witnessed. The church service allotted for this peculiar day was adopted; but, as it is the etiquette of the naval service, the holiday was also kept by an unusually liberal dinner, of which, roast beef from our Galloway ox, not yet expended, formed the essential and orthodox portion. I need not say that the rule against grog was rescinded for this day,

since, without that, it would not have been the holiday expected by a seaman. The stores of the Fury *rendered us, here, even more than the reasonable service we might have claimed; since they included minced pies, and, what would have been more appropriate elsewhere, though abundantly natural here, iced cherry brandy with its fruit; matters, however, of amusement, when we recollected that we were rioting in the luxuries of a hot London June, without the heat of a ball in Grosvenor Square to give them value, and really without any especial desire for sweetmeats of so cooling a nature. I believe that it was a happy day for all of the crew: and happy days had a moral value with us, little suspected by those whose lives, of uniformity, and of uniform ease, peace, and luxury, one or all, render them as insensible to those hard-won enjoyments, as unobservant of their effects on the minds of men. To display all our flags, was a matter of course; and the brilliancy of Venus was a spectacle which was naturally contemplated as in harmony with the rest of the day.*

That winter and the following spring, the party established good relations with the local Eskimos, while refining their dog-sledging techniques until they had become quite accomplished.

~ 1830 ~

The great disappointment for John Ross's party was that conditions were so unfavourable that summer that they managed – and that only by Herculean effort – to move the ships a mere three miles, to new winter quarters in Sheriff Harbour.[36] The excitement and ebullience of the previous Christmas was but a distant memory:

[36] Named after Felix Booth, a former Sheriff of London.

A violent storm of snow interfered with the parade of Christmas day, but all else was done according to custom.

~ 1830 ~

On 9 January 1830, less than two years after returning from his traumatic travels with Hugh Clapperton, Richard Lander sailed for Africa once again, this time in the company of his younger brother, John. The Lander brothers first met up with Pasko (Clapperton's interpreter) and then found it necessary to bribe Richard Lander's old adversary, Adele, King of Badagry, with 40 muskets and 20 signal rockets, together with promissory notes – which were never honoured. Collecting mementos of Mungo Park and braving the attentions of herds of hippopotami, King Obie's pirate hordes and the depredations of the climate, they successfully canoed down the Niger from Boussa, thus proving conclusively that the river flowed into the Bight of Benin. In late November they reached Fernando Po, a British-controlled island to the east of the Niger delta. That Christmas John Lander wrote:

Saturday, December 25th. – After a pleasant passage, we anchored this morning off Ephraim Town, in the Calebar river. The distance from Fernando Po to the north of the Calebar river is about sixty miles; and Ephraim Town is distant about fifty miles on the eastern bank. On our way up the river, my attention was attracted by something of a very extraordinary appearance hanging over the water from the branch of a tree. My curiosity was excited by it, and I was at a loss to conjecture what it was. I did not remain long in suspense, for we soon passed sufficiently near it to enable me to discover that it was the body of one of the natives suspended by the middle, with the feet and hands just touching the water. So barbarous a sight quickly reminded me that I was again among the poor deluded wretches of the coast, although I had seen nothing so bad as this on my way down to the brig Thomas, *in the river Nun. The natives of this place are pagans, in the lost depraved condition, and know nothing of Mahomedism, nor any other creed. They believe in a good spirit, who they imagine dwells in the water; and sacrifices such as that just mentioned are frequently made to him, with the idea of gaining his favour and protection. The object selected for this purpose is generally some unfortunate old slave, who may be worn out and incapable of further service, or unfit for the market; and he is thus left to suffer death either from the effects of the sun, or from the fangs of some hungry alligator or shark, which may chance to find the body. The circumstances of the hands and feet being just allowed to be immersed in the water, is considered by these deluded people as necessary, and they are thereby rendered an easier prey.*

The Lander brothers eventually arrived at Portsmouth on 9 June 1831, 'after a tedious voyage, and gladly landed with hearts full of gratitude for all our deliverances'. The following year Richard Lander was the first recipient of the Royal Geographical Society Founder's Medal 'for important services in determining the course and termination of the Niger'. Like Mungo Park, he was unable to resist the pull of the 'dark continent' and left England again in June 1832, on a commercial expedition with two steamboats to set up factories on the banks of the Niger. Also like Park, he was ambushed on a narrow stretch of the river, dying on 2 February 1834 from gangrene that set in after he had been wounded by a musket ball.

~ 1831 ~

As the weather gradually improved in Sheriff Harbour, James Clark Ross, John Ross's nephew, ventured further afield by sledge, with his primary aim the discovery of the North Magnetic Pole. On 2 June 1831 at 70° 5′ 17″ N and 96° 46′ 45″ W, he raised the union flag and 'took possession of the North Magnetic Pole and its adjoining territory in the name of Great Britain and King William the Fourth'. The discovery of the North Magnetic Pole was the high point of another pretty dismal year on the ice. That summer they managed to move little further than they had managed the previous year. Christmas was a downbeat affair, although John Ross's mind wandered widely over the wonders of preserved and frozen foodstuffs:

Christmas-day was made a holiday in all senses. In the cabin dinner, the only fact worth remarking was, a round of beef which had been in the Fury *'s stores for eight years, and which, with some veal and cooked vegetables, was as good as the day on which it was cooked.*

I know not whether the preservation of this meat, thus secured, be interminable or not; but what we brought home is now, in 1835, as good as when it went out from the hands of the maker, of whatever be his designation, the Gastronome for eternity in short, in 1823. If it can be kept so long without the slightest alteration, without even the diminution of flavour in such things as hare soup and purée of carrots, why may it not endure for ever, supposing that the vessels themselves perdurable? Often have I imagined what we should have felt had Mr. Appert's contrivance (of which, however, neither he nor his successors are the real discoverers), been known to Rome, could

we have dug out of Herculaneum or Pompeii one of the suppers
of Lucullus or the dishes of Nasidienus; the "fat paps of a sow,"
a boar with the one half roasted and the other boiled, or a
muræna fattened on Syrian slaves; or, as might have happened,
a box of sauces prepared, not by Mr. Burgess, but by the very
hands of Apicius himself. [37] *How much more would antiquaries,*
and they even more than Kitchener or Ude, have triumphed at
finding a dish from the court of Amenophis or Cephrenes, in the
tombs of the Pharaohs; have regaled over potted dainties of four
thousand years standing and have joyed in writing books on the
cookery of the Shepherd kings, or of him who was drowned in the
Red Sea. It is possible that this may yet be, some thousand years
hence, that the ever-during frost of Boothia Felix may preserve the
equally ever-during canisters of the Fury, *and thus deliver down*
to a remote posterity the dinners cooked in London during the
reign of George the Fourth?

~ 1832 ~

The *Victory*'s armourer, James Dixon, died on 10 January
1832 while, for 136 consecutive days, the thermometer did
not rise above zero. In order to extricate his stricken party,
John Ross was a man in desperate need of a plan. After three
years trapped in the ice, what were the chances of the *Victory*
sailing out the following summer? An overland journey with

---

[37] Empereur Napoléon I presented Nicolas Appert with a 12,000-franc reward
for pioneering the heat treatment and preservation of food in bottles, thus
enabling the former's army to 'march on its stomach' more effectively. After
spending the years between 71 BC and 68 BC leading Rome's legions to victory
in Pontus, the northern coast of modern Turkey, and Armenia, Lucius
Licinius Lucullus Ponticus, retired to a life of such epicurean over-
indulgence in Rome that the adjective 'Lucullan' was commonly used to
describe such excess.

the ship's boats, replenishment at bountiful Fury Beach, with the prospect of open seas beyond, seemed an altogether more attractive proposition. However, Fury Beach was 300 miles away and the ship's crew laboured for the next four months to create caches of supplies along their escape route. On 29 May the *Victory* was abandoned to its fate. By 10 June the party was well beyond the last cache and supplies were running short.

Having sent James Clark Ross ahead to ascertain that Fury Beach still held the key to their salvation, John Ross halted the rest of the party. The news was good and, although three of the *Fury*'s boats had been washed away, there was still food enough for all. By 1 July John Ross was able to write that 'we were once more at home'. 'Home' on Fury Beach was a hastily constructed dwelling called Somerset House, after the offices of the Royal Society. The ice fields opened only briefly that year and an abortive escape attempt, begun on 1 August, ended with an ignominious retreat – without the boats, abandoned at Batty Bay – to Somerset House, which they reached on 7 October. Half rations were ordered on 1 November and Christmas that year – their fourth in the Arctic – was distinctly unexciting:

> *It blew fresh on the Sunday and Monday, so as to prevent the men from going out; but a fox having been taken, served for our Christmas dinner, while the men received full allowance of meat for that day, though for them as for us, there was nothing to drink but snow water.*

It was a particularly severe winter and, with the *Fury*'s meat supplies exhausted by 1 July, it was clear that a fifth winter in the Arctic was not an option. On 8 July 1833 Somerset House was abandoned and the party reached Batty Bay four days later. It was fortunate indeed that the boats were not in need of major repairs since the carpenter, Chimham Thomas, had died five months earlier. On 14 August an escape channel finally opened in the ice and the three boats, rowing when the wind dropped away, made their escape. On 26 August 1833 they were rescued, as John Ross described:

> *About ten o'clock we saw another sail to the northward ... she was soon alongside, when the mate in command addressed us, by presuming that we had met with some misfortune and lost our ship. This being answered in the affirmative, I requested to know the name of his vessel, and expressed our wish to be taken on board. I was answered that it was "the Isabella of Hull, once commanded by Captain Ross," on which I stated I was the identical man in question, and my people the crew of the* Victory. *That the mate, who commanded this boat, was as much astonished at this information as he appeared to be, I do not doubt; while, with the usual blunderheadedness of men on such occasions, he assured me I had been dead two years.*

John Ross was indeed very much alive, as his erstwhile persecutors were about to discover. On his return to London he was lionised, not only by his fellow countrymen but throughout Europe. Having been knighted by HM King William IV, Sir John Ross repaired to his printers with almost indecent haste, in order to ensure that this new distinction was included in the soon-to-be-published narrative of the expedition. In 1834 he was the third winner of the Royal Geographical Society Founder's Medal 'for his discovery of Boothia Felix and King William Land and for his famous sojourn of four winters in the Arctic'. John Barrow was suitably

discomfited and could scarcely bear to acknowledge Sir John
Ross's very considerable achievements in any of his writings.

~ 1833 ~

In his *Narrative*, George Back described how he was drawn
back to the Arctic in search of John Ross and the *Victory*:

> *Early in the year 1832, the protracted absence of Captain (now
> Sir John) Ross, who had sailed in 1829 to the Polar regions,
> and had not afterwards been heard of, became the subject of
> general and anxious conversation. A report even reached Italy,
> where I happened to be, that he and his adventurous
> companions had perished; but, having ascertained that there
> was no other ground for this rumour than the uncertainty of
> their fate, I shortly afterwards hastened to England, with the
> intention of offering to Government my services to conduct an
> expedition in search of them.*

Sponsored by George Ross, brother of Sir John Ross and
father of James Clark Ross, George Back's intention was to
travel overland down the Great Fish River to the sea and
thence to Fury Beach. By the time that his party of twenty was
ready to depart, news of John Ross's rescue had reached
them. Nevertheless, George Back was instructed to carry on
as planned, to find out what he could. Christmas was a
modest affair:

> *Christmas-day was the appointed time for opening a soldered
> tin case, the gift of a lady of New York; but our companion Mr.
> McLeod being absent, we thought it fair to postpone the
> gratification of our curiosity till he could participate in it; and*

Mr. King and I made a cheerful dinner of pemmican ['an "iron ration" of dried meat and fat']. *Happiness on such occasions depends entirely on the mood and temper of the individuals; and we cheated ourselves into as much mirth at the fancied sayings and doings of our friends at home, as if we had partaken of the roast beef and plum-pudding which doubtless "smoked upon the board" on that glorious day of prescriptive feasting.*[38]

Having reached the mouth of the Great Fish River (soon to be renamed the Back River in his honour) the following August, their supplies were sadly too depleted for them to press on far enough to discover that Boothia Felix was in fact a peninsula, which is why John Ross and the *Victory* had found themselves trapped in a cul-de-sac. Had Back pushed on, then that discovery might have saved a lot of lives during the coming years. George Back and his party arrived back in England on 8 September 1835.

~ 1835 ~

In December 1831 HMS *Beagle*, under the command of Lieutenant Robert FitzRoy, continued her survey of the coasts of Patagonia, Tierra del Fuego and the Straits of Magellan, begun over three years earlier. This time the naturalist Charles Darwin accompanied FitzRoy. Bill Bryson wrote: 'FitzRoy, who was very odd, chose Darwin in part because he liked the shape

[38]At this date beef was the traditional Christmas fare in the north of England while goose was more popular in the south. Initially imported to Spain from Mexico by the Conquistadors, turkeys were first introduced to England by French Jesuits in the 1520s; however, they did not become the Christmas meat of choice in England until the late Nineteenth Century.

of Darwin's nose ... That Darwin was trained for the ministry was central to FitzRoy's decision to have him aboard. That Darwin subsequently proved to be not only liberal of view but less than wholeheartedly devoted to Christian fundamentals became a source of lasting friction between them.'[39] On completion of the surveying task after three-and-a-half years – famously reaching the Galapagos Islands on 15 September 1835 – the *Beagle* embarked on a world tour, calling at Tahiti, Australia, New Zealand and South Africa. On Christmas Day Charles Darwin wrote in his journal:

In a few more days the fourth year of our absence from England will be completed. Our first Christmas Day was spent at Plymouth; the second at St. Martin's Cove, near Cape Horn; the third at Port Desire, in Patagonia; the fourth at anchor in a wild harbour in the peninsula of Tres Montes; this fifth here, and the next, I trust in Providence, will be in England. We attended divine service in the chapel of Pahia [Paihia, Bay of Islands, New Zealand]*; part of the service being read in English, and part in the native language. Whilst at New Zealand we did not hear of any recent acts of cannibalism; but Mr. Stokes found burnt human bones strewed round a fire-place on a small island near the anchorage; but these remains of a comfortable banquet might have been lying there for several years. It is probable that the moral state of the people will rapidly improve. Mr. Bushby mentioned one pleasing anecdote as a proof of the sincerity of some, at least, of those who profess Christianity. One of his young men left him, who had been accustomed to read prayers to the rest of the servants. Some weeks afterwards, happening to pass late in the evening by an*

---

[39] *A Short History of Nearly Everything*, published by Random House in 2003.

*outhouse, he saw and heard one of his men reading the Bible
with difficulty by the light of the fire, to the others. After this the
party knelt and prayed: in their prayers they mentioned Mr.
Bushby and his family, and the missionaries, each separately in
his respective district.*

After a voyage lasting five years and two days, Charles Darwin
never left the shores of Britain again: *On the Origin of Species*
was published on 24 November 1859. In 1837 Robert FitzRoy
was honoured with the Royal Geographical Society Founder's
Medal 'for his survey of the coasts of South America, from the
Río de la Plata to Guayaquil in Brazil'. In 1843 he became the
second Governor of New Zealand, but was brought home
when he failed to bring the First New Zealand War to a swift
conclusion. Although Robert FitzRoy later made a significant
contribution to meteorology, and was the first to coin the
term 'weather forecast', the publication of *On the Origin
of Species* caused him the 'acutest pain' and may have
contributed to his depression – he committed suicide on 30
April 1865.

~ 1839 ~

John Lloyd Stephens, an American lawyer and diplomat who
had recently been prevented by political instability from
taking up his post as US Ambassador to Holland, wrote:
'Being entrusted by the President with a Special Confidential
Mission to Central America, on Wednesday, the third of
October, 1839, I embarked on board the British brig *Mary
Ann*, Hampton, master, for the Bay of Honduras.' He further
explained: 'My only fellow-passenger was Mr. Catherwood, an
experienced traveller and personal friend, who had passed

more than ten years of his life in diligently studying the antiquities of the Old World; and whom, as one familiar with the remains of ancient architectural greatness, I engaged, immediately on receiving my appointment, to accompany me in exploring the ruins of Central America.'[40] After visiting the ruined Mayan city of Copán – and agreeing to buy it for 50 dollars, with the intention of floating it down the river and placing it in the collection of an American museum – Stephens proceeded to Guatemala, where he spent Christmas 'at a party at Señor Zebadours':

It was Christmas Eve, the night of El Nascimiento, or birth of Christ. At one end of the sala was a raised platform, with a green floor, and decorated with branches of pine and cypress, having birds sitting upon them, and looking-glass, and sandpaper, and figures of men and animals, representing a rural scene, with an arbour, and a wax doll in a cradle; in short, the grotto of Bethlehem and the infant Saviour. Always, at this season of the year, every house in Guatimala has its nascimiento, according to the wealth and taste of the proprietor, and in time of peace the figure of the Saviour is adorned with family jewels, pearls, and precious stones, and at night every house is open, and the citizens, without acquaintance or invitation, or distinction of rank or persons, go from house to house visiting; and the week of El Nascimiento is the gayest of the year; but, unfortunately, at this time it was observed only in form; the state of the city was too uncertain to permit general

---

[40] Frederick Catherwood, an Englishman who was already well known for his drawings of archaeological sites in the Middle East, published *Views of Ancient Monuments in Central America, Chiapas and Yucatán* in 1844. He drowned when the *Arctic*, in which he was travelling from London to New York, collided with the French steamer, the *Vesta*, on 27 September 1854.

opening of house and running in the streets at night. Carrera's soldiers might enter.[41]

The party was small, but consisted of the élite of Guatimala, and commenced with supper, after which followed dancing, and, I am obliged to add, smoking. The room was badly lighted, and the company, from the precarious state of the country, not gay; but the dancing was kept up till twelve o'clock, when the ladies put on their mantas, and we all went to the Cathedral, where were to be performed the imposing ceremonies of the Christmas Eve. The floor of the church was crowded with citizens, and a large concourse from the villages around. Mr. Savage accompanied me home, and we did not get to bed till three o'clock in the morning.

The bells had done ringing, and Christmas mass had been said in all the churches before I awoke. In the afternoon was the first bullfight of the season.

Stephens concluded his travelogue with these words: 'On the thirty-first of July [1840] we arrived at New-York, being ten months less three days since we sailed, and nine without having received any intelligence whatever from our friends at home; deducting the time passed at sea, but seven months and twenty-four days in the prosecution of our work. This, I am sure, must recommend us to every true American; and here, on the same spot from which we set out together, and with but little hope of ever journeying with him again, I bid the reader farewell.' Stephens later became President of the Panama Railroad Company and died in New York on 13 October 1852, at the age of 46, apparently from the depredations of the Panamanian climate.

---

[41] At that time Rafael Carrera (1814–65) was leading a rebellion against Central American President, Francisco Morazán. In 1844 he became the first President of Guatemala.

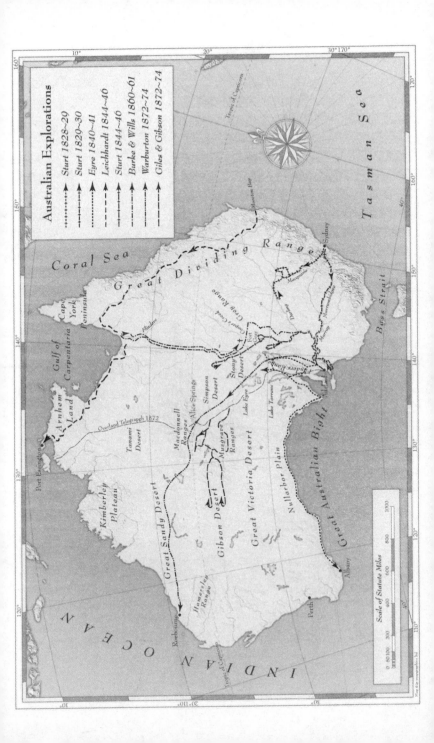

Australian Explorations

Sturt 1828–29
Sturt 1829–30
Eyre 1840–41
Leichhardt 1844–46
Sturt 1844–46
Burke & Wills 1860–61
Warburton 1872–74
Giles & Gibson 1872–74

~ 1840 ~

Edward John Eyre had emigrated from England to Australia at
the age of 19, later becoming a sheep farmer. By 13 June 1840
'the sum of £541 17s 5d [the equivalent of some £40,000
today] had been collected and paid into the Bank of Australia'
as subscriptions for an expedition with the goal of exploring
'an overland route to Western Australia'. Five days later Eyre
and his party of six white men and three Aborigines left
Adelaide, with the words of the Chairman, Charles Sturt,
ringing in their ears: 'The eyes of all the Australasian colonies
– nay, he might even say of Britain – are on the colonists of
South Australia in this matter; and he felt confident that the
result would be most beneficial, not only to this Province, but
also to New South Wales and the Australian colonies generally
– for the success of one settlement is, in a measure, the success
of the others.'[42] That Christmas, Eyre wrote in his journal:

> *Christmas day came, and made a slight though temporary break
> in the daily monotony of our life. The kindness of our friends
> had supplied us with many luxuries; and we were enabled even
> in the wilds, to participate in the fare of the season: while the
> season itself, and the circumstances under which it was ushered
> in to us, called forth feelings and associations connected with
> other scenes and with friends, who were far away; awakening,
> for a time at least, a train of happier thoughts and kindlier
> feelings than we had for a long time experienced.*

The harsh conditions and shortage of supplies forced Eyre to
send all the Europeans, with the exception of John Baxter, his

---

[42] Charles Sturt – see 1844/45.

station manager, back to Adelaide. On 25 February 1841 the reduced party of five – together with 11 pack horses and six sheep – left Fowler's Bay to find a route, suitable for cattle, across the Nullarbor Plain,[43] a journey of almost 1,000 miles. Halfway round the Great Australian Bight, two of the Aborigines began to cause trouble by refusing to work, before shooting Baxter and absconding with what little remained of the group's provisions. Eyre and Wylie struggled on for the next month, surviving by killing and eating kangaroos. They then had the good fortune to make contact with the crew of a refitting French whaler, whose English captain gave them food and new clothes as well as, most importantly, the chance to take two weeks' rest in order to recover their strength. Eyre and Wylie finally reached Albany, on the coast south-east of Perth, that July, after a journey of four-and-a-half months.

In a somewhat understated way, Edward Eyre was awarded the Royal Geographical Society Founder's Medal for 1843 'for his enterprising and extensive explorations in Australia, under circumstances of peculiar difficulty'. Australia's largest salt lake is named after him, as are Eyre Peninsula, Eyre Creek and Eyre Highway. Having served as Lieutenant-Governor of New Munster Province, New Zealand, where the villages of Eyreton and West Eyreton are named after him, he became a controversial Governor of Jamaica, where he was mired in controversy following the ruthless suppression of the so-called Morant Bay Rebellion. He died in England on 30 November 1901, at the age of 86. Wylie later received a government pension and, having forsaken exploration, wisely chose to live out his days in Albany, Western Australia.

---

[43] Nullarbor: literally, 'no trees'.

~ 1840 ~

In 1838, stimulated by French and American interest in the continent, the British Admiralty suddenly turned its attention to the Antarctic. On the pretext of determining magnetic variations in the South Polar regions, Sir John Barrow managed to obtain funding for the British Antarctic Expedition 1839–43. Having spent 17 of the previous 20 years in the Arctic, including no less than eight over-winterings – coupled with his discovery of the North Magnetic Pole – James Clark Ross was the obvious choice to lead such an enterprise. He was given two bomb ships, HMS *Erebus* and HMS *Terror*, deemed ideal for the task by virtue of their strong, capacious hulls and shallow draught.

Having set up observatories on St. Helena, at the Cape and on Kerguelen Island, the expedition received an enthusiastic welcome at Hobart, Van Diemen's Land, from an old friend, Rear-Admiral Sir John Franklin, before sailing south on 12 November 1840. Ross described Christmas:

> *Christmas-day was passed by us in a strong gale, but it did not prevent our enjoying the usual festivities of the joyous season. Constant snow and rain, which as usual attended the northerly gale, and the expectation of meeting with ice, as well as the possibility of passing new land, deterred me from running during the continuance of such unfavourable weather; we therefore hove-to under the close-reefed topsails. At noon we were in lat. 62° 10' S., and long. 170° 24' E.*

On 11 January 1841 they were the first to confirm the existence of the continent of Antarctica while, on 28 January, they saw – and named – the volcanoes, Mount Erebus and

Mount Terror. Soon afterwards they encountered what we now know as the Ross Ice Shelf, referred to by James Clark Ross simply as 'the Barrier': 'we might as well sail through the cliffs of Dover as penetrate such a mass'.[44] After spending two weeks in sailing 250 miles along the Ross Ice Shelf, Ross decided to return to Van Diemen's Land. On 6 April 1841 the *Erebus* and *Terror* anchored in the Derwent River and, by noon, Sir John Franklin was on board to welcome them back.

~ 1841 ~

On 7 July 1841 the *Erebus* and *Terror* left Hobart once again, this time equipped with three years' provisions. Ever mindful of his scientific obligations, James Clark Ross travelled via Sydney and New Zealand, setting up yet more observatories. On 23 November course was once again set for the Antarctic. By 15 December they encountered their first icebergs and, by Christmas, they were in the thick of it:

During the next few days we were much embarrassed by fogs and light winds, chiefly from the eastward, and made but little progress in the desired direction, so that we found ourselves on the twenty-fifth in latitude 66° S. and longitude 156° 14' W., and passed our Christmas-day, closely beset in the pack, near to a chain of eleven bergs, of the barrier kind, and in a thick fog the greater part of the day, with by no means a cheering prospect before us; we, nevertheless, managed to do justice to the good old English fare, which we had taken care to preserve for the occasion.

---

[44] The two Polar ice-caps are very different: while the average thickness of the Antarctic ice-cap is some 7,500 feet, the Arctic ice-cap is just ten feet thick.

Three weeks later – and still stuck in the pack – they were caught in a two-day gale and were constantly dashed against icebergs 'hard as floating rocks of granite'. On 22 February they re-encountered 'the Barrier' and, two days later, James Clark Ross gave the order to set course for the Falkland Islands. Their troubles were not yet over: on 13 March the *Erebus* and *Terror* collided as the former took desperate action to avoid an iceberg. It was only Ross's superb seamanship that enabled the disabled *Erebus* to slip between 'two perpendicular walls of ice' and the two ships eventually reached Port Louis on East Falkland on 6 April 1842.[45] The crews spent a miserable five months there, waiting for the equipment that would enable them to carry out repairs, and taking yet more observations.

~ 1841 ~

On 8 September 1842 Captain James Clark Ross, observations and repairs completed, set sail from Port Louis for Tierra del Fuego. After another spell of observation the two ships sailed once more for Antarctic waters. Their Christmas was a now-familiar combination of gales and pack ice, as Captain Ross described:

---

[45] On 15 March 1833, just two months after the British had taken possession, the Falkland Islands were visited by the *Beagle*. Charles Darwin wrote: 'After the possession of these miserable islands had been contested by France, Spain, and England, they were left uninhabited. The government of Buenos Aires then sold them to a private individual, but likewise used them, as old Spain had done before, for a penal settlement. England claimed her right and seized them. The Englishman who was left in charge of the flag was consequently murdered. A British officer was next sent, unsupported by any power: and when we arrived, we found him in charge of a population, of which rather more than half were runaway rebels and murderers.'

The gale moderated at 9 the next morning, by which time, being under the lee of Clarence Island, we found some shelter from the heavy westerly sea we had during the night experienced. Being Christmas Day, our people, as usual, had an additional allowance issued to them, and it was passed by us all cheerfully and happily, although the gale still whistled through the rigging, and we were surrounded by a great multitude of icebergs. We were indebted to the kindness of Lieutenant Governor Moody, of the Falkland Islands, for the good old English fare of roast-beef, which he provided by presenting each ship with a fine fat ox, which had been fed on one of the tussock-covered islands, for this especial occasion.

A month in the pack meant that the favourable conditions of the Antarctic summer slipped inexorably through his fingers and, on 5 March, Ross set course for Simon's Bay, South Africa, anchoring there on 4 April 1843. After a journey home via St. Helena, Ascension Island and Rio de Janeiro, he recorded:

The shores of Old England came into view at 5.20am on the 2nd of September, and we anchored off Folkestone at midnight of the 4th. I landed early the next morning, and immediately proceeded to the Admiralty, where I met the most gratifying reception from Lord Haddington, Sir William Gage, and my highly valued friends, Admiral Beaufort and Sir John Barrow. A few days after my arrival in London, I had not only the gratification of receiving the Founder's Medal awarded to me by the Council of the Royal Geographical Society of London, but that which afforded me, if possible, still greater pleasure, was the receipt of the Gold Medal of the Royal Geographical Society of Paris.

Just seven weeks after his return to England, James Clark Ross married Ann Coulman, immediately promised her that his exploring days were over and settled down to the life of a country gentleman near Aylesbury. The following year he was knighted and received an honorary degree from Oxford University. The expedition was an undoubted success, advancing the cause of science in a number of different areas. Captain Francis Crozier was elected a Fellow of the Royal Society in recognition of his outstanding work on magnetism but, tragically, gave no such commitments concerning his future plans. Edward Sabine, a veteran of both John Ross's and William Parry's first expeditions of 1819–20, interpreted the expedition's magnetic observations in the *Philosophical Transactions* of the Royal Society while Joseph Dalton Hooker, the expedition's resident botanist on the *Erebus*, wrote *Flora Antarctica*.[46]

~ 1844 ~

Ludwig Leichhardt, who was born in Trebatsch, Prussia on 23 October 1813, went to Australia in 1842 in order to study the geology, flora and fauna.[47] On 1 October 1844 he left Jimbour Station, the last European outpost, some 150 miles north-west of Brisbane, with a party of nine others on an expedition to find a new route to Port Essington, near Darwin. They took with them 17 horses, 16 bullocks, 550 kilograms of flour, 90 kilograms of sugar, 40 kilograms of tea and 10 kilograms of gelatine. Two

---

[46] Both these gentlemen died in their 95th year: General Sir Edward Sabine KCB FRS died on 26 May 1883 while Sir Joseph Hooker GCSI OM FRS MD died on 10 December 1911.

[47] Ludwig Leichhardt is the eponymous hero of *Voss*, by Nobel Prize-winning, Australian author Patrick White.

members of the party turned back soon after the start while the naturalist, John Gilbert, was killed in 'an avalanche of spears' by the Kokopera people of the Cape York Peninsula. Of that Christmas, Leichhardt recorded in his journal:

We returned to Brown's Lagoons, and entered our camp just as our companions were sitting down to their Christmas dinner of suet pudding and stewed cockatoos. The day was cloudy and sultry; we had had a heavy thunder-storm on Christmas eve.

Seven exhausted men finally reached Port Essington in January 1846 after a journey of more than 3,000 miles. They had travelled through good country, naming the Dawson, Mackenzie, Isaacs, Suttor and Burdekin Rivers, as well as the Expedition and Peak Ranges. The survivors of the party then travelled by sea back to Sydney, where they received a hero's welcome, at least partly because no one had expected to see them again. The following year Ludwig Leichhardt was awarded the Royal Geographical Society Patron's Medal 'for explorations in Australia, especially for his journey from Moreton Bay to Port Essington'. In 1848 he set off on another expedition: from the Darling Downs, across central Australia, to Perth. On 3 April 1848 Leichhardt wrote from McPherson's Station on the Cogoon River to Captain Phillip Parker King RN, of Tahlee, Port Stephens:

Seeing how much I have been favoured in my present progress, I am full of hope that our Almighty Protector will allow me to bring my darling scheme to a successful termination.

The party of six white men and two black boys – accompanied by an astonishing menagerie comprising 180 sheep, 270 goats, 40 bullocks, 15 horses and 13 mules – was never seen again. Despite nine major expeditions between 1852 and 1938, no trace of them has been discovered.

~ 1844 /45 ~

In 1826 Captain Charles Napier Sturt of the 39th Regiment of Foot escorted a group of convicts to Sydney in the *Mariner*. Soon bored with regimental soldiering, Captain Sturt started to explore the inner regions of the then-unknown continent, eventually becoming 'the virtual founder of South Australia'.[48] In November 1828 he penetrated the marshes of the Upper Macquarie, reaching an unfamiliar river, which he promptly named the Darling, after the Governor, Ralph Darling. The following year he explored the Murrumbidgee and Murray rivers, in a whaleboat initially carried overland in sections, covering over 2,000 miles by land and by water. In August 1844 Sturt embarked on his own most significant journey, into the centre of the continent, where he expected to find an inland sea. That December he wrote in his journal:

On the morning of the 24th, about 5 A.M., I was roused from sleep by an alarm in the camp, and heard a roaring noise as of a heavy wind in that direction. Hastily throwing on my clothes, I rushed out, and was surprised to see Jones's dray on fire; the tarpaulin was in a blaze, and caused the noise I have mentioned. As this dray was apart from the others, and at a distance from any fire, I was at a loss to account for the accident; but it appeared that Jones had placed a piece of lighted

---

[48] *The Dorsetshire Regiment* by C. T. Atkinson, published by Oxford University Press in 1946.

cowdung under the dray the evening before, to drive off the mosquitos, which must have lodged in the tarpaulin and set it on fire. Two bags of flour were damaged, and the outside of the medicine chest was a good deal scorched, but no other injury done. The tarpaulin was wholly consumed, and Jones lost the greater part of his clothes, a circumstance I should not have regretted if he had been in a situation to replace them.

Finding no inland sea, but only the Stony and Simpson Deserts, the party turned back. The following Christmas, as Sturt's party was slowly making its way back to Adelaide, he wrote in his journal:

The 25th being Christmas Day, I issued a double allowance to the men, and ordered that preparations should be made for pushing down the river on the following morning.

Of his explorations in Australia, Sturt concluded:

I sought that career, not, I admit, without a feeling of ambition as should ever pervade a soldier's breast, but chiefly with an earnest desire to promote the public good, and certainly without any hope of any other reward than the credit due to the successful enterprise.

In 1847 Charles Napier Sturt was awarded the Royal Geographical Society Founder's Medal 'for explorations in Australia, and especially for his journey fixing the limits of Lake Torrens and penetrating into the heart of the continent to lat. 24° 30′ S, long. 138° 0′ E'. He later served as Chief Secretary of South Australia, lived at 'The Grange' (now the Charles Sturt Museum), in the Adelaide suburb of

Grange, returned to England in 1853 and died at Cheltenham on 16 June 1869, having been awarded – but never invested with – a KCMG.

~ 1846 ~

Although Sir John Barrow insisted – as well the Second Secretary to the Admiralty might – that ships were the only answer, the directors of the Hudson's Bay Company had other ideas.[49] Having garnered knowledge of weather conditions, diet and the challenge of self-sufficiency by living close to – rather than aloof from – the native people, they favoured the flexibility offered by overland expeditions. No-one was better suited to lead such an expedition than Dr. John Rae: after qualifying as a surgeon in Edinburgh in 1833, he had spent the next ten years at Moose Factory on Hudson Bay. Among other essential skills, he learned how to make and use snowshoes, how to hunt and then preserve caribou, how to get the best performance from sledges and how to construct shelters. During just two months in 1844 he walked no less than 1,200 miles on his snowshoes, thus earning himself the Inuit name Aglooka, or 'he who takes long strides'.

In 1846 John Rae led a characteristically well-prepared expedition to explore the western shore of Hudson's Bay, as far as Repulse Bay and to the Fury and Hecla Strait, ostensibly with a view to mapping the coast for the Hudson's Bay

---

[49] The Hudson's Bay Company is one of the oldest trading companies in the world, having incorporated on 2 May 1670 by British royal charter. With a monopoly on the fur trade in Hudson Bay and surrounding region, the trappers (voyageurs) travelled into the interior, bringing their pelts to the factories (called after the 'factors', who were in charge) on the shores of the Bay itself, or on the banks of the rivers that flowed into the Bay.

Company but, equally inevitably, with half an eye on the discovery of the North West Passage. He described their Christmas festivities:

Christmas-day was passed very agreeably, but the weather was so stormy and cold that only a very short game at foot-ball could be played. Short as it was, however, it was sufficiently amusing, for our faces were every moment getting frost-bitten either in one place or another, so as to require the continual application of the hand; and the rubbing, running about, and kicking the ball all at the same time, producing a very ludicrous effect.

Our dinner was composed of excellent venison and a plum-pudding, with a moderate allowance of brandy punch to drink a health to absent friends.

Not only was Rae's expedition, which returned on 6 September 1847, successful in achieving its objectives but, just as importantly, it was notably within both budget and the allotted timescale. However, the Royal Navy did not heed these lessons. As we shall see, Rae often triumphed over the nautical competition during the next few years.

~ 1850 ~

Nelson Kingsley, the third son of Nathan Kingsley of New Milford, Connecticut, went to seek his fortune in the California Gold Rush, beginning his journal on 8 February 1849. Almost two years later he wrote over Christmas:

24th tues A clear fine day worked at clearing off again today – shall not wash much this week. Tonight being so pleasant, and the night before Christmas I almost wish myself among my friends at home. I can however imagine how they are doing. The choirs are chanting hymns of praise. Many an able sermon is written to enlighten the minds of the people, and all is bustle & confusion, sleigh bells perhaps are pealing forth their merry tones, to many joyous hearts, but here am I away from all these lovely scenes toiling away, for what, that which may yet afford me comfort at some future day. Still I but little know what use may be made of it. Therefore I will spend as little time here as possible. Therm 30 morn 59 noon 48 eve

25th wed Christmas Day A beautiful day, not a cloud hardly to be seen, I hardly think they have had a more pleasant day in New England. I worked on the bar at clearing off today and have now got so that tomorrow we shall wash. My luxuries today are limited as far as eatables is concerned for breakfast fried-ham – doughnuts & crackers & cheese &c for dinner about the same, and for supper stewed Oysters which were fresh & nice they come from Boston, in sealed tins and taste as fresh and delicious as they would have done the day they were put up. The evening I spent at Mr. Potters – was entertained with a Mr. Smith from New Haven [the home of Yale University]. *He came from there the last of September. He gave me all the news from there which was highly entertaining. The people of New Haven are all alive with internal improvements – other public buildings have been built with internal improvements – churches have been remodelled & new ones built – other public buildings have been built of superior beauty & taste – durability &c. All in the short space that I have been absent, the place will seem odd says he when you return to see the changes that have transpired, he seemed like an old friend, tho' I have never before spoke with him. Many a pleasant "yarn was spun" during the evening which made the time pass away pleasantly. Therm 50-55-43*

Thursday 26th Worked at washing today, got 13 ounces 11 dollars in amalgam. George Brisco worked with us today. The greatest days work that has been done yet on the bar was done by Mr. Turner, with 6 men in all, he took over 80 ounces in amalgam this is some & no mistake. Therm 29-54-38

According to the editor of the journal: 'Upon or shortly after his return to Connecticut in 1851, Nelson married the young lady to whom he was engaged prior to his departure for the West, and the following year, 1852, he died without issue.'

~ 1852 ~

Despite the fact that he was now 59-years-old, Rear-Admiral Sir John Franklin was now appointed to command yet another expedition to find the North West Passage and, on 19 May 1845, together with 133 officers and men, sailed from Greenhithe in HMSs *Erebus* and *Terror*.[50] What followed became one of the Victorian era's more enduring mysteries: Franklin's ships were last seen moored to an iceberg in the north of Baffin Bay on 26 July 1845 by Captain Dannett of the whaler *Prince of Wales*.

Although the Admiralty took some persuading that the Franklin expedition may have met with disaster, the machinery eventually swung into action. On 12 April 1848 Sir James Clark Ross was the first to leave, breaking his promise

---

[50] While Sir John Franklin succeeded Sir James Clark Ross in command of HMS *Erebus*, Captain Francis Crozier FRS was once again in command of HMS *Terror*. In 1828, following a triumphant return the previous year from his second Arctic expedition – in which his party travelled 2,000 miles and mapped 610 miles of previously unexplored coastline – Sir John Franklin was knighted by HM King George IV.

to his new wife by taking command of HMSs *Enterprise* and *Investigator*. While Sir John Barrow still lived, there was a degree of coordination in these efforts. However, after his death on 23 November 1848, things rapidly deteriorated: 'in the season of 1850, there were in all fifteen vessels taking part in the search for Sir John Franklin's expedition: eleven on the Baffin Bay side, and four on the Behring Strait side, besides one or two land parties'. Two of these ships, the *Advance* and the *Rescue*, were there as a result of an appeal from Lady Franklin to US President Zachary Taylor: paid for by New York philanthropist, Henry Grinnell, they were manned by US Navy volunteers. Even 73-year-old Sir John Ross was in on the act, in command of the 90-ton *Felix*, once again funded by his old sponsor, Sir Felix Booth. To enliven matters still further, prizes were back on the agenda: £20,000 for rescuing Franklin, £10,000 for finding his ships and £10,000 for being the first to cross the North West Passage.

In the spring of 1852 Rear-Admiral Sir Edward Belcher was given charge of the Franklin Search Expedition, which consisted of no less than five ships: the *Assistance*, the *Resolute*, the *Intrepid*, the *Pioneer*, the supply ship *North Star* and a boat, the *Forlorn Hope*. In the light of what actually happened, some of these brave names now appear faintly ironic. Within weeks of their arrival, Sir Edward Belcher's ships became ice-bound, at which point the inappropriateness of the appointment of such an unimaginative martinet became abundantly clear, to everyone but himself. Belcher described that first Christmas on HMS *Assistance*, before everything went horribly wrong:

> *On presentation of wine by the leading petty officer, I addressed a*
> *few words to them, expressive of my satisfaction, and reminding*

them that the roast beef then smoking before them was "Her Majesty's own," requested that due honour should be accorded to the health of "Her Most Gracious Majesty Victoria, God bless her! and all the Royal Family." This over, I gave the health of "The 'Pioneers', and may their enjoyment never be less than this Christmas!" I now returned, to preside, at noon, over the opening festival of my own crew. Here too I found all the luxuries, not forgetting roast beef and plum-puddings.

By the winter of 1853/54 Belcher's command was rapidly disintegrating, with his ships trapped in the ice and his subordinates proving increasingly immune to his orders. The following August, Belcher abandoned four of his five ships and sailed for home in *North Star*. Later court-martialled – and controversially acquitted – he devoted the rest of his life to writing, and trying to justify his actions.

There was an interesting postscript. On 16 September 1855, Captain James Buddington of the American whaler, *George Henry*, was astonished to come across the *Resolute* in the Davis Strait, some 1,200 miles from where she had been abandoned: 'A deathlike silence and a dread repose. For a year and four months no human foot had trod the deck of that deserted ship.' She was purchased for US$40,000 by the United States Congress, completely refitted and, on 17 December 1856, presented to HM Queen Victoria as a token of peace. In 1880, after the *Resolute* was finally broken up, Victoria returned the favour by presenting US President Rutherford S. Hayes with a desk made from its timbers. The original desk is still in use in the Oval Office and there is a replica desk at the Jimmy Carter Library and Museum, Atlanta, Georgia.

~ 1853 ~

After the return to England on 28 October 1849 of Captain Sir James Clark Ross from his abortive search for Franklin's expedition, principally due to widespread scurvy, Captain Richard Collinson was given command of those same ships – with himself in HMS *Enterprise* and Captain Robert McClure in HMS *Investigator* – and tasked with approaching the Franklin search area from the west, through the Bering Strait. Instead of working together, the two ships' captains ended up competing with one another. Having decided that the North West Passage, and not Franklin, was the more worthy goal, Captain McClure disobeyed orders and seized the initiative by entering the Arctic region a year earlier than Captain Collinson, who turned back and over-wintered at Hong Kong. Though separated, both ships eventually became trapped in the ice and their rescue was part of Sir Edward Belcher's initial brief. Although they never met up, Collinson kept coming across the tracks of his subordinate, which did not greatly please him. A scouting party from HMS *Resolute* eventually discovered the *Investigator* and, reluctantly convinced of the absolute necessity of abandoning his ship, McClure and his crew made their way to the *Resolute*, trapped off Dealy Island, thus becoming the first Europeans to complete the North West Passage, albeit partly on foot.

Meanwhile Collinson, who penetrated deeper into the Arctic than McClure, came within 30 miles of the route taken by Franklin's expedition. He also obtained a copper alloy adze head, formerly the property of Franklin's men, from the Inuit at Cambridge Bay on Victoria Island. With the crew of the *Investigator* safely gathered in – although he had no way of knowing it – Collinson described that Christmas in his journal:

We had no venison for our Christmas fare, but I issued half a pound of pemmican and a pint of wine, upon which the people made a very good dinner, and fared nearly as well as the officers, as our private stocks were now almost exhausted. The dogs came in for the greater portion of the hind leg of a bear, which had been reserved for the occasion, but although fresh, was pronounced not to equal either Sir J. Richardson's admirable pemmican or Mr. Gamble's excellent preserved meat.

After Collinson had successfully shepherded HMS *Enterprise* back to England in May 1855, he became even more displeased with the turn of events, as Parliament awarded £5,000 (worth almost £350,000 today, according to the increase in the retail price index – or more than £3 million if average earnings are used as the comparison) to the insubordinate McClure, with £5,000 to his officers and crew. They decided not to award the whole £15,000, as agreed in 1818, as the terms implied an approach from the Atlantic side only. While the Royal Geographical Society awarded McClure its Patron's Medal in 1854 'for his discovery of the North West Passage', Collinson had to wait another four years before he received the Society's Founder's Medal 'for discoveries in the Arctic regions'.

Meanwhile, in April 1854, the first firm intelligence concerning the fate of Franklin's party had been obtained from the Inuit by John Rae, the Hudson's Bay Company's overland specialist. Having offered a reward for artefacts, he obtained Sir John Franklin's badge of the Royal Guelphic Order. [51] Although he

[51] A Hanoverian Order of Knighthood, awarded to Sir John Franklin on 25 January 1836 – this badge is now in the collection of the National Maritime Museum, Greenwich.

had not visited the grave site, Rae received £10,000 from the Government for 'settling' Franklin's fate.[52] This infuriated the indomitable Jane, Lady Franklin, who promptly funded a private expedition. Commanded by Captain Francis Leopold McClintock, the 177-ton screw-driven yacht, *Fox*, sailed from Aberdeen on 2 July 1857. Almost two years later, on 25 May 1859, they found the first body on King William Land. Soon afterwards they found a cairn containing a standard Admiralty message form in a metal canister. There were two messages, the second being written round the margins of the first. The latter revealed that, on 26 April 1848, with Franklin and 23 others already dead, the remainder were starting for the Back River. None of them survived: according to the Inuit, they died as they walked.[53] Over a ten-year period, over £700,000 and more than US$250,000 had been expended on attempts to save, or find out what had happened to, the Franklin party.

The plinth of Rear-Admiral Sir John Franklin's statue in Waterloo Place, London – which also carries the names of the crew members on brass panels – bears the inscription: *They forged the last link with their lives.* As we now know, that was not the case: Franklin did not discover the

---

[52] John Rae was the first to establish that King William Land was an island – thus completing the last piece of the North West Passage jigsaw – and is commemorated by Rae Strait, which separates King William Land from the mainland. However, Rae never managed to navigate the Passage. That distinction lies with Roald Amundsen, who sent a telegram from Eagle City, Alaska on 5 December 1905, announcing to the world that he and six companions had successfully negotiated the North West Passage in the *Gjøa*, a 70-foot, square-sterned, 48-ton sloop with a shallow draught.

[53] Numerous theories have since been advanced concerning the deaths of the Franklin party, with lead poisoning from the solder used to seal their canned provisions proving one of the most enduring.

secret of the North West Passage. 'Lord Franklin' is a once well-known ballad:

> *In Baffin's Bay where the whale-fish blow*
> *The fate of Franklin no man can know*
> *The fate of Franklin no man can tell*
> *Lord Franklin with the fish doth dwell.*

A brief glance at the map confirms that, for all their vanity, bombast, stupidity and petty rivalries, these brave men have permanent memorials: Franklin Strait, Collinson Peninsula, Fury and Hecla Strait, Parry Bay, McClure Strait, Richard Collinson Inlet, Rae Strait, Back River, James Ross Strait and Belcher Channel.

~ 1854 ~

After enjoying a peripatetic upbringing in Europe, Richard Francis Burton was sent down from Trinity College, Oxford for betting on the horses, before obtaining a commission in the army of the Honourable East India Company. Having been one of the first European non-believers to visit Mecca and Medina, in 1853, he was soon afterwards attracted by the prospect of being the first European to visit the city of Harar in Somalia. Undeterred by the death threat for any infidel who tried, Burton received official sanction for his mission. Of that Christmas he wrote:

The ghostly western hills seemed to recede as we advanced over the endless rolling plain. Presently the ground became broken and stony, the mules stumbled in deep holes, and the camels could scarcely crawl along. As we advanced our Widads, who, poor devils! had been "roasted" by the women all day on account of their poverty, began to recite the Koran with might, in gratitude for having escaped many perils. Night deepening, our attention was riveted by a strange spectacle; a broad sheet of bright blaze, reminding me of Hanno's fiery river, swept apparently down a hill, and, according to my companions, threatened the whole prairie. These accidents are common: a huntsman burns a tree for honey, or cooks his food in the dry grass, the winds rises and the flames spread far and wide. On this occasion no accident occurred; the hills, however, smoked like a Solfatara for two days.

About 9 P.M. we heard voices, and I was told to discharge my rifle lest the kraal be closed to us; in due time we reached a long, low, dark line of sixty or seventy huts, disposed in a circle, so as to form a fence, with a few bushes – thorns being hereabouts rare – in the gaps between the abodes. The people, a mixture of Girhi and Gudabirsi Bedouins, swarmed out to gratify their curiosity, but we were in no humour for long conversations. Our luggage was speedily disposed in a heap near the kraal, the mules and camels were tethered for the night, then, supperless and shivering with cold, we crept under our mats and fell asleep. That day we had ridden nearly fifteen hours; our halting place lay about thirty miles from, and 240° south-west of, Koralay.

On 2 January 1855 Burton finally reached the walled city of Harar, with which he was distinctly unimpressed. After meeting the Amir, he wrote: 'I was under the roof of a bigoted prince whose least word was death; amongst a people who detest foreigners; the only European who had ever passed over their inhospitable threshold, and the fated instrument of their future downfall.' The threat was not carried out but the group was harried throughout their journey to the coast.

Later that same year Burton saw action in the Crimean War, before disputing the discovery of Lake Tanganyika with John Hanning Speke. In 1859 he was awarded the Royal Geographical Society Founders' Medal 'for his various exploratory enterprises, and especially for his perilous expedition with Captain J. H. Speke to the great lakes in Eastern Africa'.

~ 1860 ~

The government of South Australia offered a £2,000 (now worth some £135,000) prize for the first crossing of the country from south to north. There were two competing expeditions: one led by policeman, Robert O'Hara Burke, and the other by freemason, John McDouall Stuart. Burke's party of 18 left Royal Park, Melbourne on 20 August 1860, accompanied by 22 horses and 25 camels, the first time that an Australian expedition had used camels.[54] Having first established a base camp at Cooper's Creek, approximately the halfway point, Burke, his second-in-command, surveyor William John Wills, and two companions left there to continue north on 16 December. On Christmas Eve Wills wrote:

We took a day of rest on Gray's Creek to celebrate Christmas. This was doubly pleasant as we had never in our most sanguine moments anticipated finding such a pleasant oasis in the desert. Our camp was really an agreeable place, for we had all the advantages of food and water attending a position on a large creek or river, and were at the same time free of the

---

[54] Between 1860 and 1907 some 10,000 camels were shipped to Australia from India and Palestine: with over 400,000 feral camels now living in the outback, aerial culls have begun.

annoyance of the numberless ants, flies, and mosquitoes that
are invariably met with amongst timber or heavy scrub.

On Christmas Day they continued their journey:

We left Gray's Creek at half-past four A.M. and proceeded to
cross the earthy rotten plains in the direction of Eyre's Creek. At
a distance of about nine miles we reached some lines of trees and
bushes which were visible from the top of the sand ridge at
Gray's Creek … The smoke of a fire indicated the presence of
blacks, who soon made their appearance and followed us for
some distance, beckoning us away to the north-east … The day
being very hot and the camels tired from travelling over the
earthy plains, which by-the-by are not nearly so bad as those at
the head of Cooper's Creek, we camped at one P.M.., having
traced the creek up about five miles, not counting the bends.

On 9 February 1861 the party of four finally reached the delta
of the Flinders River, the longest river in Queensland,
although they were unable to penetrate the swamps and
reach the northern coast of Australia. During the return
journey Charles Gray died of dysentery on 17 April and the
remaining three reached Cooper's Creek four days later, only
to find it deserted. Their extra supplies had never been
delivered and, furthermore, the base party, having given up
hope of ever seeing them again, had left just eight hours
earlier. The day they spent burying Gray was to prove fatal.
Although they tried to survive on cakes made from the spore-
producing tissues of *nardoo*, a local aquatic fern, Burke
eventually died of starvation on 1 July 1861. Wills died a few
days later, leaving John King as the only survivor, having been
cared for by aborigines until a rescue party finally arrived.

~ 1861 ~

Lucie Duff Gordon was born in 1821, the only daughter of John Austin, author of *The Province of Jurisprudence Determined*, a seminal work, and his wife, Sarah, who translated books from German into English. Her parents' friends were the radicals and free thinkers of the day: among others, the Carlyles, Sydney Smith, Jeremy Bentham and John Stuart Mill. At Kensington Old Church on 16 May 1840 she married Sir Alexander (Alick) Duff Gordon, an impoverished Treasury official; they had three children. Having contracted tuberculosis, she was advised by her doctor to seek a kinder climate than that of Esher, where their house was known to members of their circle as 'The Gordon Arms'. On 17 September 1861 she arrived in South Africa but, finding Cape Town cold, soon moved up-country to Caledon, from where she wrote to Alick on 29 December:

I am beginning now really to feel better: I think my cough is less, and I eat a great deal more. They cook nice clean food here, and have some good claret, which I have been extravagant enough to drink, much to my advantage. The Cape wine is all so fiery. The climate is improving too. The glorious African sun blazes and roasts one, and the cool fresh breezes prevent one from feeling languid. I walk from six till eight or nine, breakfast at ten, and dine at three; in the afternoon it is generally practicable to saunter again, now the weather is warmer. I sleep from twelve till two. On Christmas-eve it was so warm that I lay in bed with the window wide open, and the stars blazing in. Such stars! they are much brighter than our moon. The Dutchmen held high jinks in the hall, and danced and made a great noise … Christmas-day was the hottest day – indeed, the only hot day we have had – and I could not make it out at all, or fancy you all cold at home.

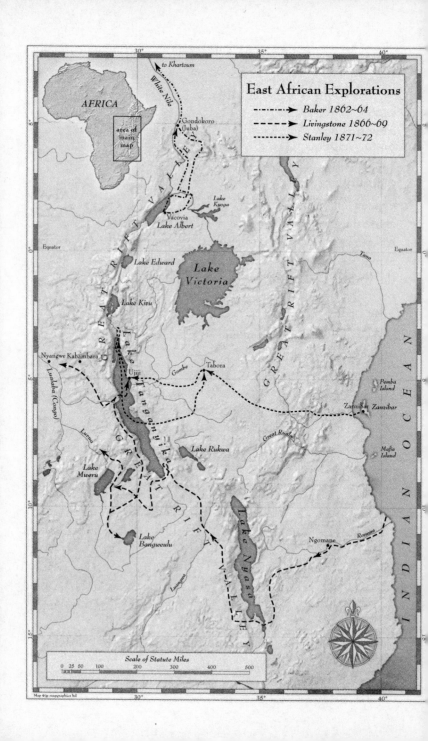

~ 1862 ~

After spending eight years in Ceylon as a young man, Samuel White Baker then travelled widely in Central Europe, before embarking on an expedition to Central Africa 'to discover the sources of the Nile, with the hope of meeting the East African expedition under Captains Speke and Grant somewhere about the Victoria Lake'. After spending a year on the Sudan-Abyssinia border, during which time he also learned Arabic, Samuel Baker left Khartoum on 19 December 1862 to sail up the White Nile. That Christmas he wrote:

25th Dec. – The Tokroori boy, Saat, is very amiable in calling all the servants daily to eat together the residue from our table; but he being so far civilized, is armed with a huge spoon, and having a mouth like a crocodile, he obtains a fearful advantage over the rest of the party, who eat soup by dipping kisras (pancakes) into it with their fingers. Meanwhile Saat sits among his invited guests, and works away with his spoon like a sageer (water-wheel), and gets an unwarrantable start, the soup disappearing like water in the desert.[55] *A dead calm the greater portion of the day; the river fringed with mimosa forest. These trees are the Soont (Acacia Arabica) which produce an excellent tannin: the fruit, "garra," is used for that purpose, and produces a rich brown dye: all my clothes and the uniforms of my men I dyed at Khartoum with this "garra". The trees are about eighteen inches in diameter and thirty-five feet high; being in full foliage, their appearance from a*

---

[55] Saat died of plague at the beginning of May 1865, just three days from Khartoum on the return journey. According to Baker: 'It was a happy end – most merciful, as he had been taken from a land of iniquity in all the purity of a child converted from Paganism to Christianity. He had lived and died in our service a good Christian.'

distance is good, but on closer approach the forest proves to be a desolate swamp, completely overflowed; a mass of fallen dead trees protruding from the stagnant waters, a solitary crane perched here and there upon the rotten boughs; floating water-plants massed together, and forming green swimming islands, hitched generally among the sunken trunks and branches; sometimes slowly descending with the sluggish stream, bearing, spectre-like, storks thus voyaging on nature's rafts from lands unknown. It is a fever-stricken wilderness – the current not exceeding a quarter of a mile per hour – the water coloured like an English horse-pond; a heaven for mosquitoes and a damp hell for man; fortunately, this being the cold season, the winged plagues are absent. The country beyond the inundated mimosa woods is of the usual sandy character, with thorny Kittur bush. Saw a few antelopes. Stopped at a horrible swamp to collect firewood. Anchored at night in a dead calm, well out in the river to escape malaria from the swamped forest. This is a precaution that the men would neglect, and my expedition might suffer in consequence.[56] *Christmas Day!*

Two months later Baker met up with Speke and Grant at Gondokoro and, armed with information from them, was the first European to lay eyes on the Lake Albert N'yanza (now more commonly known as Lake Albert), on 14 March 1864. For this discovery, together with his exploration of the sources of the Nile, Baker was knighted. Appointed pasha by the

[56] Samuel Baker was not exaggerating. Of their departure from Khartoum, he wrote: 'On passing the steamer belonging to the Dutch ladies, Madame van Capellan, and her charming daughter, Mademoiselle Tinné, we saluted them with a volley, and kept up a mutual waving of handkerchiefs until out of view; little did we think that we should never meet those kind faces again, and that so dreadful a fate would envelop almost the entire party.' Of seven Europeans in that party, only Mademoiselle Tinné survived the rigours of the climate.

ambitious Khedive Ismail in 1869, Sir Samuel Baker led a military expedition in the regions of the lower Nile and was subsequently appointed governor-general of the province of Equatoria. After being succeeded by Charles George Gordon (of Khartoum) in 1874, Baker bought an estate at Sandford Orleigh in Devon, wrote at length about his adventures, and died on 30 December 1893.

~ 1864 ~

By late summer 1862 Lucie Duff Gordon had returned to England, but only briefly, for she soon sought a 'cure' at Eaux-Bonnes in the Pyrénées. The visit was not a great success and she later wrote: 'I hear the drip, drip, drip of Eaux-Bonnes when I am chilly in my sleep.' It was thought that Egypt might be more suitable so that is where she went – without her husband but with her maid-servant Sally – in the autumn of 1862. The following year Duff Gordon wrote to her mother:

On the Nile
Friday, December 23, 1864

Dearest Mutter,
Here I am again between Benisouef and Minieh, and already better for the clean air of the river and the tranquil boat life; I will send you my Christmas Salaam from Siout. While Alick was with me I had as much to do as I was able and could not write for there was much to see and talk about. I think he was amused but I fear he felt the Eastern life to be very poor and comfortless. I have got so used to having nothing that I had quite forgotten how it would seem to a stranger.
I am quite sorry to find how many of my letters must have

been lost from Luxor; in future I shall trust the Arab post which certainly is safer than English travellers. I send you my long plaits by Alick, for I had my hair cut short as it took to falling out by handfuls after my fever, and moreover it is more convenient Turkish hareem fashion.

Please tell Dean Stanley how his old dragoman Mahommed Gazawee cried with pleasure when he told me he had seen Sheykh Stanley's sister on her way to India, and the 'little ladies knew his name *and shook hands with him, which evidently was worth far more than the backsheesh. I wondered who 'Sheykh' Stanley could be, and Mahommed (who is a darweesh and very pious) told me he was the* Gassis *(priest) who was* Imám *(spiritual guide) to the son of our Queen, 'and in truth,' said he, 'he is* really *a Sheykh and one who teaches the excellent things of religion, why he was kind even to his horse! and it is of the mercies of God to the English that such a one is the Imám of your Queen and Prince.' I said laughing, 'How does thou, a darweesh among Muslims, talk thus of a Nazarene priest?' 'Truly oh Lady,' he answered, 'one who loveth all the creatures of God, him God loveth also, there is no doubt of that.' Is any one bigot enough to deny that Stanley has done more for real religion in the mind of that Muslim darweesh than if he had baptised a hundred savages out of one fanatical faith into another.* [57]

There is no hope of a good understanding with Orientals until Western Christians can bring themselves to recognise the common faith contained in the two religions, the real *difference consists in all the class of notions and feelings (very important ones, no doubt) which we derive – not from the Gospels at all –*

---

[57] The Very Reverend Arthur Penrhyn Stanley (1815–81), Dean of Westminster, had travelled in Egypt and Palestine in 1852 and was later instrumental in the founding of the Palestine Exploration Fund.

but from Greece and Rome, and which of course are altogether
wanting here.

~ 1866 ~

David Livingstone was born at the village of Blantyre Works,
Lanarkshire on 19 March 1813 and left school at the age of
ten to work in the local cotton mill. Through his own efforts,
he finally qualified for more formal education at the age of
23, attending classes at Anderson's College, Glasgow. He was
accepted by the London Missionary Society in 1838,
qualifying as a doctor two years later. On 31 July 1841 he
reached the mission station at Kuruman, Bechuanaland,
established over 30 years earlier by Robert Moffat. During the
next 11 years, Dr. Livingstone, soon joined by his wife, Mary,
Moffat's daughter, set up a succession of stations, moving
deeper and deeper into unknown country.

After his family sailed home from Cape Town in June 1852,
Livingstone embarked on his travels in central southern
Africa, seeking a settlement free from the tsetse fly. Having
left Luanda, 200 miles south of the mouth of the Congo, he
crossed the continent from east to west, in the process
becoming, on 17 November 1855, the first European to set
eyes on Mosi-oa-Tunya, or 'the Smoke that Thunders', which
he renamed the Victoria Falls. Having reached Quilimane,
200 miles north of the mouth of the Zambezi, on 20 May
1856, he was welcomed in England that December as
a conquering hero. In February 1858, Livingstone was
appointed 'Her Majesty's consul at Quilimane for the eastern
coast and the independent districts in the interior, and
commander of an expedition for exploring eastern and
central Africa'. He spent the next six years following the brief,

in the course of which his wife died at Shupanga on 27 April 1862 and their son, Robert, was killed fighting for the Union cause at the Battle of Gettysburg in July 1863.

In 1866 Dr. Livingstone was persuaded to return to Africa to lead yet another expedition, this time with two goals: the suppression of slavery through civilising influences and the discovery of the watershed between the Lakes Nyasa and Tanganyika. Accompanied only by his loyal African servants, the situation had become fairly desperate by Christmas:

23rd December. – Hunger sent us on; for a meat diet is far from satisfying: we all felt very weak on it, and soon tired on a march, but to-day we hurried on to Kavimba, who successfully beat off the Mazitu.[58] It is very hot, and between three and four hours is a good day's march. On sitting down to rest before entering the village we were observed, and all the force of the village issued to kill us as Mazitu, but when we stood up the mistake was readily perceived, and the arrows were placed again in their quivers. In the hut four Mazitu shields show that they did not get it all their own way; they are miserable imitations of Zulu shields, made of eland and water-buck's hides, and ill sewn.

A very small return present was made by Kavimba, and nothing could be bought except at exorbitant prices. We remained all day on the 24th haggling and trying to get some grain. He took a fancy to a shirt, and left it to his wife to bargain for. She got the length of cursing and swearing, and we bore it, but could get

---

[58] The Mazitu are described by H. Rider Haggard, author of *King Solomon's Mines*, as 'a numerous and warlike people of bastard Zulu blood'.

only a small piece for it. We resolved to hold our Christmas some other day, and in a better place. The women seem ill-regulated here – Kavimba's brother had words with his spouse, and at the end of every burst of vociferation on both sides called out, "Bring the Muavi! bring the Muavi!" or ordeal.[59]

Christmas-day, 1866. – No one being willing to guide us at Moerwa's, I hinted to Kavimba that should we see a rhinoceros I would kill it. He came himself, and led us on where he expected to find these animals, but we saw only their footsteps. We lost our four goats somewhere – stolen or strayed in the pathless forest, we do not know which, but the loss I felt very keenly, for whatever kind of food we had, a little milk made all right, and I felt strong and well, but coarse food hard of digestion without it was very trying. We spent the 26th in searching for them, but all in vain.

~ 1868 ~

Having spent two years exploring the lakes of Central Africa – Nyasa, Bangweulu and Mweru – Dr. Livingstone's party was now making its way towards Lake Tanganyika:

25th December, Christmas Day. – We can buy nothing except the very coarsest food – not a goat or a fowl – while Syde, having plenty of copper, can get all the luxuries.[60] *We marched past Mount Katanga, leaving it on our left, to the River Kapéta, and slaughtered a favourite kid to make a Christmas dinner. A*

---

[59] Drinking the juice of the goho plant was an ordeal undergone by women.

[60] Syde bin Habib, an Arab trader.

111

trading-party came up from Ujiji; they said that we were ten camps from Tanganyika. They gave an erroneous report that a steamer with a boat in tow was on Lake Chowambé [Lake Albert] – an English one, too, with plenty of cloth and beads on board. A letter had come from Abdullah bin Salem, Moslem missionary at Mtésa's, to Ujiji three months ago with this news.

By then just 'a ruckle of bones', Livingstone arrived at Ujiji on 14 March 1869.

~ 1868 ~

On 25 January 1869 Lucie Duff Gordon wrote to her husband, Alick, from Assouan:

We have been here ten days, and I find the air quite the best for me. I cough much less, only I am weak and short of breath. I have got a most excellent young Reis for my boat, and a sailor who sings like a nightingale, indeed he is not a sailor at all, but a professional Cairo singer who came up with me for fun. He draws crowds to hear him, and at Esneh the congregation prayed for me in the mosque that God might reward me for the pleasure I had provided for them. Fancy desiring the prayers of this congregation for the welfare of the lady who gave me her opera-box last Saturday. If prayers could avail to cure I ought to get well rapidly. At Luxor Omar killed the sheep he had vowed, and Mustapha and Mohammed each killed two, as thank-offerings for my life, and all the derweeshes held two great Zikrs in a tent pitched behind the boat, and drummed and chanted and called on the Lord for two whole nights; and every man in my boat fasted Ramadan severely, from Omar and the crew to the little boys. I think Darfour was the most meritorious of all, because he has such a Gargantuan appetite, but he fasted his thirty days bravely and rubbed his little nose in the dust energetically in prayer.

On Christmas Day I was at Esneh, it was warm and fine, and I made fantasia and had the girls to dance. Zeyneb and Hillaleah claim to be my own special Ghazawee, *so to speak my* Ballerine da camera, *and they did their best. How I did long to transport the whole scene before your eyes – Ramadan warbling intense lovesongs, and beating on a tiny tambourine, while Zeyneb danced before him and gave the pantomime to his song; and the sailors, and girls, and respectable merchants sat* pêle-mêle *all round on the deck, and the player on the rabab drew from it a wail like that of Isis for the dead Osiris. I never quite know whether it is now or four thousand years ago, or even ten thousand, when I am in the dreamy intoxication of a real Egyptian fantasia; nothing is so antique as the Ghazawee – the* real *dancing girls. They are still subject to religious ecstasies of a very curious kind, no doubt inherited from the remotest antiquity. Ask any learned pundit to explain to you the* Zar *– it is really curious.*

Now that I am too ill to write I feel sorry that I did not persist and write on the beliefs of Egypt in spite of your fear that the learned would cut me up, for I honestly believe that knowledge will die with me which few others possess. You must recollect that the learned know books, and I know men, and what is still more difficult, women.

Having spent seven years living in Upper Egypt, the longest time that a European had spent there until that time, Lucie Duff Gordon died in her boat *Urania*, moored off Boulak, Cairo on 14 July 1869. Egypt was changing fast: that same year the Suez Canal was opened and the first Cook's tour steamed up the Nile. She recorded a world that was fast vanishing and – more unusually – recognized the fact.

~ 1869 ~

On 22 January 1861 at the Church of Our Lady of the Assumption in Warwick Street, London, Richard Burton married Isabel Arundell. Regarding large weddings as 'a most barbarous and indelicate exhibition', he wore rough tweeds. Isabel Burton was now on her way to join her husband, who had taken a consular post at Damascus:

We spent Christmas Eve as our last night on board. In the evening we went in for snapdragon and other festivities of the season, and tried to be as merry as we could. The ship could not go into the harbour of Alexandria at night; it has a dangerous entrance; so we sent up our rockets and blue-lights, and remained outside the lighthouse till dawn. On Christmas Day morning I first set my foot on Eastern ground. We steamed into the harbour of Alexandria slowly; everybody was going on to India except me, and I landed. The first thing I did was to go straight to a telegraph office and pay nineteen shillings and sixpence for a telegram to Richard at Beyrout (Beirut), *which of course arrived there after I did. I cannot say that I was struck with Alexandria; in point of fact, I mentally called it "a hole" in vulgar parlance. I went to the* Hôtel de l'Europe, *a second-rate hotel, though one of the best in Alexandria. It was not so bad as might have been expected. In the afternoon we made a party up to see Pompey's Pillar and Cleopatra's Needle and the bazars and other things.*[61] *But I am bound to say that, on the whole, I thought Alexandria "neither fish, flesh, fowl, nor good red herring." It was a sort of a jumble of Eastern and*

---

[61] Cleopatra's Needle refers to the obelisks later erected in London and New York, in 1878 and 1881 respectively.

Western, and the worst of each. The only amusing incident which happened to me there was when two dragomans got up a fictitious quarrel as to who should take me to the bazars. Of course they appealed to me, and I said, "You may both come, but I shall only pay one." Whereupon they fastened upon each other tooth and nail, tore each other's clothes, and bit each other's cheeks. These two, though I never suspected it at the time, were, it appeared, in the habit of thus dealing with ladies and missionaries and amiable English tourists; and they always got up this farce, because, to avoid a street fight, the kindhearted looker-on would generally employ and pay them both, and perhaps give them a tip in addition to calm them down. But I innocently did the right thing without knowing it. I had so often seen negroes fight with knives in Brazil that the spectacle of two dragomans biting each other's cheeks appeared to me to be supremely ridiculous. I laughed, and waited patiently until one of them pretended to be very much hurt. Then turning to the other, I said, "You seem the better man; I will take you"; and they were both very much crestfallen. I spent the evening alone in my small room at the hotel. A strange Christmas truly.

Richard Burton later translated *The Kama Sutra of Vatsayayana* from Sanskrit and *The Arabian Nights* from Arabic and eventually came to speak no less than 25 languages. He was knighted in 1886 and died at Trieste on 20 October 1890. Having converted to Roman Catholicism on his deathbed, Sir Richard Burton lies in a life-size stone tent, designed by Lady Burton, in the churchyard of St. Mary Magdalen's Roman Catholic Church in suburban Mortlake, London. She died on 22 March 1896 and the two coffins can be seen, side-by-side, through a window in the back of the 'tent'.

~ 1871 ~

In 1869 the *New York Herald* financed an expedition to find
Dr. David Livingstone, of whom nothing had been heard for
over five years. The reporter and adventurer, Henry Morton
Stanley, was given the daunting task. After travelling over
700 miles in 236 days, Stanley memorably found Livingstone
at Ujiji on the shores of Lake Tanganyika on 27 October
1871. Livingstone recorded the momentous encounter in
his journal:

> But when my spirits were at their lowest ebb, the good
> Samaritan was close at hand, for one morning Susi came
> running at the top of his speed and gasped out, "An
> Englishman! I see him!" and off he darted to meet him. The
> American flag at the head of a caravan told of the nationality
> of the stranger. Bales of goods, baths of tin, huge kettles, cooking
> pots, tents, &c., made me think "This must be a luxurious
> traveller, and not one at his wit's end like me." ... The news he
> had to tell to one who had been two full years without any
> tidings from Europe made my whole frame thrill. The terrible
> fate that had befallen France, the telegraphic cables successfully
> laid in the Atlantic, the election of General Grant, the death of
> good Lord Clarendon – my constant friend, the proof that Her
> Majesty's Government had not forgotten me in voting 1000l.
> for supplies, and many other points of interest, revived emotions
> that had lain dormant in Manyuema.[62]

---

[62] The comprehensive defeat of France and the Siege of Paris during the
Franco-Prussian War 1870–71. George William Frederick Villiers, 4th Earl of
Clarendon, was British Foreign Secretary on three occasions and also served
as Lord Privy Seal, Chancellor of the Duchy of Lancaster, President of the
Board of Trade and Lord Lieutenant of Ireland.

Two months later Stanley's initial elation at the success of his mission had subsided somewhat:

On the 20th of December the rainy season was ushered in with heavy rain, thunder, lightning, and hail; the thermometer falling to 66 degrees Fahrenheit. The evening of this day I was attacked with urticaria, or "nettle rash", for the third time since arriving in Africa, and I suffered a woeful sickness; and it was the forerunner of an attack of remittent fever, which lasted four days. This is the malignant type, which has proved fatal to so many African travellers on the Zambezi, the White Nile, the Congo, and the Niger. The head throbs, the pulses bound, the heart struggles painfully, while the sufferer's thoughts are in a strange world, such only as a sick man's fancy can create. This was the fourth attack of fever since the day I met Livingstone. The excitement of the march, and the high hope which my mind constantly nourished, had kept my body almost invincible against an attack of fever while advancing towards Ujiji; but two weeks after the great event had transpired my energies were relaxed, my mind was perfectly tranquil, and I became a victim.

Christmas came, and the Doctor and I had resolved upon the blessed and time-honoured day being kept as we keep it in Anglo-Saxon lands, with a feast such as Ujiji could furnish us. The fever had quite gone from me the night before, and on Christmas morning, though exceedingly weak, I was up and dressed, and lecturing Ferajji, the cook, upon the importance of this day to white men, and endeavouring to instil into the mind of the sleek and pampered animal some cunning secrets of the culinary art. Fat broad-tailed sheep, goats, zogga and pombe, eggs, fresh milk, plantains, singwe, fine cornflour, fish, onions, sweet potatoes, &c., &c., were procured in the

117

Ujiji market, and from good old Moeni Kheri. But, alas! for
my weakness. Ferajji spoiled the roast, and our custard was
burned – the dinner was a failure. That the fat-brained
rascal escaped a thrashing was due only to my inability to lift
my hands for punishment; but my looks were dreadful and
alarming, and capable of annihilating any one except
Ferajji. The stupid, hard-headed cook only chuckled, and I
believe he had the subsequent gratification of eating the pies,
custards, and roast that his carelessness had spoiled for
European palates.

In his journal, Livingstone wrote simply: '26th December –
Had but a sorry Christmas yesterday.'

~ 1872 ~

After setting set off from Ujiji together, Stanley left Livingstone
on 15 March 1872, promising to send fresh bearers and
supplies. While Stanley returned initially to London, and then
to New York, gaining a major scoop with the headline –
LIVINGSTONE SAFE – in the 2 May 1872 edition of the *New York
Herald*, the subject of all this curiosity simply waited patiently at
Umyamwezi for five months for re-supply before continuing
on his travels. That Christmas he wrote:

25th December, Christmas Day. – I thank the good Lord for the
good gift of His Son Christ Jesus our Lord. Slaughtered an ox,
and gave a fundo and a half to each of the party. This is our
great day, so we rest. It is cold and wet, day and night. The
headman is gracious and generous, which is very pleasant
compared with awe, awe, and refusing to sell, or stop to speak,
or show the way.

David Livingstone was soon struck down with yet another dose of fever and, for the last two weeks, he had to be carried by litter to the edge of Lake Bangweulu. On 27 April 1873 he made the last entry in his journal: 'Knocked up quite and remain – recover. Sent to buy milch goats. We are on the banks of R Molilamo.' David Livingstone died on 1 May 1873 but his loyal bearers then wrapped up his body and carried it – together with all his papers and scientific instruments – across southern Africa to Zanzibar. The journey of over 1,000 miles took nine months. On 18 April 1874 the remains of Dr. David Livingstone were laid to rest in Westminster Abbey.

~ 1873 ~

Two wealthy patrons, Sir Thomas Elder and Walter (later Sir Walter) Hughes, funded an expedition to find an overland route from Adelaide to Perth. The 'terra incognita' of over 500,000 square miles was described to the Royal Geographical Society as 'the greatest blank on the face of the globe – polar regions excepted'. This was the first Australian expedition to be equipped entirely with camels as beasts of burden. Expedition leader, Colonel Peter Egerton Warburton, had clearly learnt from the experiences of his predecessors: 'No horse could have lived with us. Camels alone can travel over any but boggy ground. Horses alone are useless where there is no feed and little water, but excellent where both are abundant. I, however, have never found any such country.' Having left Adelaide on 21 September 1872, they spent their second Christmas waiting for help:

We cannot but draw a mental picture of our friends in Adelaide sitting down to their Christmas dinner, whilst we lie sweltering on the ground starving, and should be thankful to have the pickings out of any pig's trough. This is no exaggeration, but literal truth. We cut out three bee-holes to-day, but found no honey in any of them. No sign of Lewis. If he is not here by the close of Sunday next, I shall be obliged to suppose he has gone to Roebourne, in which case there can be no hope of his return for the next three weeks, and, except God grant us His help, we cannot live so long on our present supply ... We fancied we should find many opossums in the gum-trees, but have not seen one. We have fish close to us, but though we deprive ourselves of the entrails of a bird as bait, they will not take it. We eat everything clean through, from head to tail. Prejudiced cooks may not accept my advice, but I am quite satisfied all birds ought to be cooked whole, extracting what you please afterwards. We omitted the latter operation, but this is a matter depending on circumstances. Our last Christmas at Alice Springs was miserable enough, as we then thought, but the present one beats it out and out.

The group eventually reached Roebourne, some 900 miles north of Perth, on 26 January 1874. Of the 17 camels, only two survived. That November Warburton returned to England for the first time in 40 years, was awarded the Royal Geographical Society Patron's Medal 'for his successful journey across the previously unknown western interior of Australia' and picked up a CMG from HM Queen Victoria; however, finding the climate 'insupportable', he returned to Adelaide just a month later. Two mountain ranges, a river and a beetle are named after him.

~ 1873 ~

In 1872 Ernest Giles set out to cross Western Australia but, although he discovered Mount Olga,[63] the Finke River and *livistona mariae,* the Central Australian fan palm, his party of three was forced to turn back due to lack of water. On 4 August 1873 he began his second attempt with a new companion, Alfred Gibson, who had no previous experience of the outback. They got no further than Fort Muller before making camp for the summer. In the Arctic it was the cold and dark that led explorers to hibernate for the winter; in the Australian outback, the extreme heat was the problem. Of Christmas that year Giles wrote:

On the 23rd, when we arrived, Gibson informed us that the natives had been extremely troublesome, and had thrown several spears and stones down from the rocks above, so that he and Jimmy had had to defend themselves with firearms. Our bough-house was a great protection to them, and it appeared also that these wretches had hunted all the horses away from their feeding ground, and they had not been seen for three days, and not having come up to water all the time we were away. At four P.M. we had our afternoon earthquake, and Gibson said the shock had occurred twice during our absence. The hostility of the natives was very annoying in more senses than one, as it would delay me in carrying out my desire to visit the new and distant ranges north. Christmas had been slightly anticipated by Gibson, who said he had made and cooked a Christmas pudding,

---

[63] Named after Queen Olga of Württemberg, it lies little more than 30 miles from Uluru or Ayers Rock.

and that it was now ready for the table. We therefore had it for dinner, and did ample justice to Gibson's cookery. They had also shot several rock-wallabies, which abound here. They are capital eating, especially when fried; then they have a great resemblance to mutton … And now comes Thursday, 25th December, Christmas Day, 1873. Ah, how the time flies! Years following years, steal something every day; at last they steal us from ourselves away. What Horace says is, Eheu fugaces anni labuntur postume, postume *– Years glide away, and are lost to me, lost to me … Our last discharge drove away the enemy, and soon after, Jimmy came with all the horses. Gibson shot a wallaby, and we had fried chops for our Christmas dinner. We drew from the medical department a bottle of rum to celebrate Christmas and victory. We had an excellent dinner (for explorers), although we had eaten our Christmas pudding two days before. We perhaps had no occasion to envy any one their Christmas dinner, although perhaps we did. Thermometer 106° in the shade.*

In April, Giles and Gibson set off into the desert. Gibson's horse died after just three days and, since progress was so slow, Gibson went back for help, mounted on Giles's horse. He was never seen again and, as its first white victim, the Gibson Desert was named after him. Ernest Giles survived, after a 60-mile walk, carrying a 45-pound keg of water.

~ 1875 ~

The British Arctic Expedition 1875–76 had as its principal object the discovery of the North Pole. Captain George Nares was expedition leader in the *Alert* while Henry Stephenson commanded the *Discovery*.[64] Having left Portsmouth on 29 May 1875, the two ships sailed as far as Lady Franklin Bay on Ellesmere Island, from where the *Alert* proceeded 50 miles further north, only to become ice-bound for 11 months. During a three-week sledging expedition, Lieutenant William Henry May was badly frostbitten, with the result that his left big toe had to be amputated. In his memoirs he wrote:

A la Julienne soup is the potage we favour,
And soles fried au naturel *serve us for fish.*
We have cutlets and green peas of elegant flavour –
Beef garnished with mushrooms – a true English dish.

Then a mountain of beef from our cold Greenland valleys,
Overshadowing proudly boiled mutton hard by;
Till our appetite, waning, just playfully dallies
With a small slice of ham – then gives in with a sigh.

For lo! a real British plum-pudding doth greet us,
And a crest of bright holly adorns its bold brow;
While the choicest mince-pies are yet waiting to meet us;
Alas! are we equal to meeting them now?

So we drink to our Queen; and we drink to the Maiden.
The Wife, or the Mother, that holds us most dear;
And may we and our Consort sail home richly laden
With the spoils of success, 'ere December next year.

---

[64] George Nares was a veteran of the ill-fated HMS *Resolute* from the Franklin Search Expedition 1852–54.

He admitted that 'I am afraid they [the mess caterer's menus] read a good deal better than they were'. Two sledging parties set off from *Alert* on 3 April but, although they covered 521 miles in 60 days, they were still only 73 miles from their ship and 400 miles from the North Pole, a new 'Farthest North' record. By August 1876 over 40 per cent of the crew members on the two ships were suffering from scurvy, from which four men eventually died. With the safety of his crews in mind, Nares turned for home. Although he had to suffer the indignity of an inquiry, he did receive the compensation of a knighthood, together with the Royal Geographical Society Founder's Medal.

~ 1878 ~

Born in Helsinki on 18 November 1832, when the Grand Duchy of Finland was still part of the Russian Empire, Adolf Erik Nordenskiöld was dismissed from his post at the Imperial Alexander University in his home city for daring to express anti-imperialist views at the time of the Crimean War. After three geological expeditions to Spitzbergen had whetted his appetite, he attempted to discover the North East Passage, along the northern coasts of Europe and Siberia, across the Chukchi Sea, through the Bering Strait and into the Bering Sea. Having left Karlskrona on 22 June 1878, initial progess was swift until the *Vega* became trapped in drift ice on 28 September at Pitlekaj, off the Chukchi Peninsula, north-eastern Siberia, just two days' sailing from the northern entrance to the Bering Strait. The expedition leader described Christmas:

Christmas Eve was celebrated in the usual northern fashion. We had indeed neglected, as in the Expedition of 1872–73, to take with us any Christmas tree. But instead of it Dr. Kjellmann prevailed on our Chukch friends to bring with dog-sledges willow-brushes from the valleys lying beyond the mountains to the south. By means of these a bare driftwood stem was converted into a luxuriant, branchy tree which, to replace the verdure, was clothed with variegated strips of paper, and planted in the 'tweendecks, which after our enclosure in the ice had been arranged as a working room, and was now set in order for the Christmas festivities, and richly and tastefully ornamented with flags. A large number of small wax-lights, which we had brought with us for the special purpose, were fixed in the Christmas tree, together with about two hundred Christmas boxes purchased or presented to us before our departure. At six o'clock in the afternoon all the officers and crew assembled in the 'tweendecks, and the drawing of lots began, now and then interrupted by a thundering polka round the peculiar Christmas tree. At supper neither Christmas ale nor ham was wanting. And later in the evening there made their appearance in the 'tweendecks five punchbowls, which were emptied with songs and toasts for King and Fatherland, for the objects of the Expedition, for its officers and men, for the families at home, for relatives and friends, and finally for those who decked and arranged the Christmas tree, who were the sailors C. Lundgren and O. Hansson, and the firemen O. Ingelsson and C. Carlström.

The other festivals were also celebrated in the best way, and at midnight before New Year's Day the new year was shot in with sharp explosive-shell firing from the rifled cannon of the Vega, *and a number of rockets thrown up from the deck.*

It was almost ten months before the ice released them from its grip and the *Vega* was able to continue her voyage.

Nordenskiöld and his crew created a sensation when they reached Yokohama in Japan on 2 September 1879: they had safely negotiated the North East Passage. After a prolonged stay, during which Nordenskiöld met the Meiji Emperor and attended numerous celebrations and dinners, the *Vega* finally sailed from Yokohama on 11 October 1879.

~ 1879 ~

During a leisurely cruise home, the *Vega* called at Hong Kong, Singapore and Ceylon, before setting course for the coaling station at Aden. Adolf Nordenskiöld described their second Christmas away:

> *We started from Point de Galle on the 22nd December, and arrived at Aden on the 7th January. The passage was tedious in consequence of light winds or calms. Christmas Eve we did not celebrate on this occasion, tired as we were of entertainments, in such as festive way as at Pitlekaj, but only with a few Christmas-boxes and some extra treating. On New Year's Eve, on the other hand, the officers in the gun-room were surprised by a deputation from the forecastle clad in pesks as Chukches, who came, in good Swedish, mixed with a few words of the Pitlekaj lingua franca not yet forgotten, to bring us a salutation from our friends among the ice of the north, thanks for the past and good wishes for the coming year, mixed with Chukch complaints of the great heat hereaway in the neighbourhood of the equator, which for fur-clad men was said to be altogether unendurable.*

The *Vega* sailed through the Suez Canal and along the length of the Mediterranean, calling later at Lisbon,

London and Copenhagen before finally reaching Stockholm on 24 April 1880. Nordenskiöld was created a Swedish baron (known as Nils) and appointed Knight Grand Cross of the Order of the North Star. The Nordenskiöld Crater on Mars is named in honour of Nils Adolf Erik Nordenskiöld, who died at Dalbyö, Sweden on 12 August 1901.

~ 1879 ~

Having visited the Arctic regions in the *Juniata* during the 1873 search for the missing *Polaris*,[65] the experiences of Lieutenant-Commander George Washington DeLong, United States Navy, later developed into a theory that it might be possible to reach the North Pole in a ship specially strengthened to drift in the pack ice. DeLong persuaded James Gordon Bennett Jr.,[66] proprietor of the *New York Herald*, to finance an expedition to test his hypothesis. In 1878 Bennett purchased HMS *Pandora*, renamed her the *Jeannette* after his sister and turned her over to the US Navy while still paying the

---

[65] The *Polaris* expedition could serve as a blue-print for the 'heroic' age of exploring: Charles Francis Hall received a grant of US$50,000 from the US Congress to lead an expedition to the North Pole; the *Polaris* sailed into winter quarters in Thank God Harbour (now Hall Bay on the coast of Greenland on 10 September 1871; suffering from vomiting and delirium, Hall died on 8 November, having accused several of the ship's company of poisoning him; the *Polaris* is crushed in the ice; the crew split into two groups and are eventually rescued by whalers, but only because the Inuit led them to safety. When Hall's body was exhumed in 1968 it was found to contain large quantities of arsenic.

[66] He gave universal usage to the term 'Gordon Bennett': one of his many excesses was to relieve himself in the fireplace of his future in-laws at his engagement party – the marriage was called off.

operating costs.[67] In July 1879 the *Jeannette* sailed for the Bering Strait and first entered the ice near Herald Island on 6 September. That Christmas DeLong wrote in his journal:

> *Christmas Day! This is the dreariest day I have ever experienced in my life, and it is certainly passed in the dreariest part of the world. And yet we (or rather I) ought not to complain, for it is something to have had no serious mishap up to this time. We tried to be jolly, but did not make any grand success of it until dinner time, when fore and aft we had such a grand banquet that we were for a time lifted out of and beyond the contemplation of our surroundings. We should have been comparatively happy were it not that one of our mess did not appear at the dinner table. At four P.M. the crew, headed by Boatswain Cole, came aft into the cabin to wish us all a merry Christmas, and to invite us into the deck-house to hear a little music. We thanked them for their courtesy and went to the deck-house, where they played music, sang songs, and Alexey gave us a native dance. At all events the crew seemed to have a merry Christmas.*

~ 1880 ~

During the whole of the 1880, while the *Jeanette* continued to drift with the pack ice, the crew occupied themselves by making scientific occupations, maintaining their ship and hunting polar bears and seals. Although things were still proceeding according to plan, DeLong wrote that 'we tried to

---

[67] The second HMS *Pandora*: the first was sent to apprehend the *Bounty* mutineers, of whom they found just fourteen. They were duly locked in 'Pandora's Box' but four drowned when the *Pandora* was wrecked off the Great Barrier Reef on 28 August 1791.

be cheerful, and make Christmas Eve rather less dreary than many of our days now seem.' They put a brave face on matters the following day, as DeLong described:

The day was made as acceptable as possible fore and aft, by the providing of a good dinner from our resources. And I think we may refer to our bills of fare with pardonable pride. Our mince pies were a work of art; though they were made from pemmican and flavored by a bottle of brandy, they were as delicate to the taste as if compounded from beef fresh from market. Hot whiskey punch in the evening fore and aft brought an agreeable close to our second Christmas in the pack.

On 31 December, DeLong confided to his journal: 'The last day of the year and I hope all our trials and tribulations have gone with it.' Sadly, it was not to be. The following June the ice briefly showed signs of breaking up – but it was a false dawn. On 12 June the ice floes returned with renewed force, crushing the *Jeanette*'s hull. With the goal of reaching the Lena River Delta, 700 miles away on the north Siberian coast, the crew retrieved what supplies they could and dragged three boats over the ice to open water.

For the next three months they struggled southwards until, on 12 September, the three boats became separated in a storm. One was never seen again while the other two landed, unbeknownst to one another, on opposite sides of the Lena River Delta. The party of eleven commanded by George W. Melville, later Engineer-in-Chief, soon met up with friendly locals and was led to safety. Meanwhile DeLong, having despatched two seamen to seek help, waited in vain for a rescue party. DeLong's last journal entry was: 'Sunday Oct 30 – 140th day – Boyd and Gertz died during night – Mr. Collins dying.' Their bodies, together with DeLong's journal, were not discovered until March 1882. While the remaining 12 members of DeLong's party died, the two seamen sent ahead, William F. C. Nindemann and Louis P. Noros, both survived.

~ 1881 ~

On 26 July 1861, at the age of 17, Augustus Washington Greely enlisted in the Union Army as a volunteer private. After the Civil War he served in the Signal Corps, developing a particular interest in meteorology. The outgoing Hayes Administration had voted US$25,000 for the Lady Franklin Bay Expedition, the purpose of which was to explore Greenland and Grinnell Land, making notes of the weather and the tides over a planned two-year period.[68] On 7 July 1881 Lieutenant Augustus W. Greely, three other officers, twenty enlisted men and two Inuits sailed from St. John's, Newfoundland, in the *Proteus*, establishing themselves at Fort Conger on Ellesmere Island on 26 August. That first Christmas was a happy one, as Greely recalled:

Christmas morning came clear and cold, with a temperature of freezing mercury, which moderated later in the day. The calm air, unstirred by wind, made exercise tolerable, and all sought the harbor-floe for a long walk, in hopes of a marvellous appetite.

At 10 A.M. the Psalms for Christmas were read, to which I added as appropriate the second selection, consisting of the 139th

[68] The new President, James A. Garfield, who had absolutely no interest in polar exploration, had been shot just five days earlier, and lingered until 19 September 1881. In 1851 Grinnell Land was named after Henry Grinnell, the philanthropist who paid for the first American Arctic Expedition that took part in the search for Sir John Franklin and his missing men.

and 140th Psalms. This reading was supplemented by the singing of a hymn and the doxology, led off by Lieutenant Kislingbury. I remember no service in all our Arctic experiences which so affected and impressed the men, unless it was that at our first burial in the winter, at Sabine. Our thoughts and tenderest feelings could not but go out to those we had left behind, with doubts and fears as to whether it fared well or ill with them, never distrusting but their hearts were with us in our Arctic Christmas.

Christmas falling on Sunday, no amusements of any kind were attempted, but everyone waited with interest and a certain impatience for the dinner, which was as elaborate as our stores would permit. The menu for the dinner was as follows: Mock-turtle soup, salmon, fricasseed guillemot, spiced musk-ox tongue, crab-salad, roast beef, eider-ducks, tenderloin of musk-ox, potatoes, asparagus, green corn, green peas, cocoanut-pie [sic], jelly-cake, plum-pudding with wine-sauce, several kinds of ice-cream, grapes, cherries, pineapples, dates, figs, nuts, candies, coffee, chocolate. Egg-nog was served to the party in moderate quantities, and an extra allowance of rum was also issued in celebration of the day. The candies, plum-pudding and cigars were the most appreciated, not only for the satisfaction that they afforded the taste, but as being gifts from thoughtful friends. The cigars came from an army lady who knew the weaknesses of the rank and file for the consoling weed, and the candies were from a leading confectioner of New York City.

On the 26th the men were busy in the preparation for a variety show, which was set for that evening, as Christmas had fallen on a Sunday. The Lime-Juice Club announced that they would perform at the Dutch Island Opera House for one night only, and that dog-chariots could be ordered at 10 P.M. The admission fee was in tobacco, the current coin of Grinnell Land.

The first act was a representation of an Indian Council, which ended with a war-dance. Nine of the party participated in this scene, which was admirably rendered. Most of the actors had served in the far West, and some had spent months continuously in Indian camps, and so were thoroughly familiar with the parts they portrayed. I doubt very much if a more realistic representation of the wild red-man was ever presented in the Arctic Circle, if elsewhere.

A female impersonation followed, by Schneider, which afforded amusement for the party, but particularly so to the Eskimo. Schneider had provided himself at the Greenland ports with the entire costume of the Eskimo belle, and being a small man, was able to squeeze himself into the garments. As he appeared on the scene with his elaborate make-up and closely-shaven face, one was struck by the excellent resemblance to the Inuit belles whom we had seen in lower latitudes. In his amowt, *or woman's hood, he brought the largest of his charges, one of the Grinnell Land puppies, who was nearly frightened to death by the appearance which greeted his first advent into polite society.*

The following spring the North Greenland Sledge Party, which comprised Lieutenant James Lockwood, Sergeant David Brainard and Greenland hunter and dog-driver, Frederick Christiansen, achieved a new 'Farthest North' of latitude 83° 24′ N and longitude 40° 46′ W on 13 May 1882, thus beating Commander Albert Markham's 1876 record. In all they covered 1,072 miles on a journey that took 60 days. That September, although they didn't know it at the time, the Lady Franklin Bay Expedition's problems began when their supply ship, the *Neptune*, was forced by ice to turn back, when still 300 miles away of Fort Conger.

~ 1883 ~

There was no immediate crisis, because the expedition was stocked with provisions for a two-year sojourn on Grinnell Land. However, by August 1883, with winter closing in once again, Augustus Greely decided to put his contingency plan into effect and led the party south. After a 34-day drift on the ice they eventually reached Cape Sabine, where they built a modest 25-foot by 18-foot stone house, with an upturned boat for a roof, but with headroom of only four feet. In his journal Greely described a more modest Christmas feast:

December 25th. – Christmas. Temperature, -34.8° (-37° C.). Lieutenant Kislingbury thirty-six years old. Our breakfast was a thin pea-soup, with seal-blubber and small quantity of preserved potatoes. That of the other mess was similar to it. Later two cans of cloudberries were served to each mess, and at half past one o'clock Long and Frederick commenced cooking dinner, which consisted of a seal stew, containing seal-blubber, preserved potatoes, and bread, flavored with pickled onions; then came a kind of rice pudding, with raisins, seal-blubber, and condensed milk. Afterward we had chocolate, followed later by a punch made of a gill of rum and a quarter of lemon, to each man.

The idea of scanting ourselves for a comfortable Christmas had borne good fruit, and is now heartily commended by all. There was a great deal of kindly feeling and good-will shown to-day, and a general desire was expressed to heal over any old wounds or uncharitable feeling. Late in the evening the records left by Lieutenant Garlington and Mr. Clay's letter were read. Everybody was required to sing a song or tell a story, and

pleasant conversation, with the expression of kindly feelings,
was kept up until midnight. We had Danish, Eskimo, German,
and English songs. One event of the evening was the reading of
a birthday bill of fare, which had been made up by the party for
future birthdays.

With food running desperately short, the first death from starvation occurred on 17 January 1884. What followed was horrific: a steady stream of deaths, the execution of one of the party for stealing food and even, as was unearthed only later, evidence of cannibalism. Although seven expedition members were still alive when the crew of the *Thetis* reached them on 22 June 1884, one of them, Sergeant Joseph Elison, died just three days later, after having had all his limbs amputated in a desperate attempt to save his life. Feeling spurned by an ungrateful nation, an embittered Greely later wrote:

No man of the party has received promotion, except such
temporary advancement as my personal urging could secure.
Two men, with broken health, have adventured their private
fortunes; and one, a most self-sacrificing, soldierly, temperate,
and loyal man, lies, as these lines are penned, helpless in a city,
hospital, aided by private charity, his pension not even awarded.

Even the meagre allowances originally promised for Arctic
service have not been fully paid, and the widows of the dead are
generally as yet unrecognized.

Our great country in these days asks not in vain for its sons
to venture their lives for any idea which may subserve its
interests or enhance its greatness. I trust that posterity may
never mourn the decadence of that indomitable American spirit
which in this generation fought out to the bitter end its great
civil war, and made it seem an easy thing in time of peace to

*penetrate the heart of Africa, to perish in the Lena Delta, to die
at Sabine, or to attain the Farthest North.*[69]

Greely is unique in rising through the ranks from volunteer
private to major-general in the US Army. On 27 March 1935,
his 91st birthday, he received the Congressional Medal of
Honor, one of only four explorers to have been honoured in
this way, out of a total of 3,460 recipients. The others are Charles
A. Lindbergh, Richard E. Byrd and Floyd Bennett (see below).

~ 1893 ~

Fridtjof Nansen was just 21 when he first sailed in the waters
off Greenland in a sealing ship; six years later he was a
member of a party that crossed the Greenland icefield on skis
from east to west. Some three years after George W. DeLong's
Jeanette had been wrecked off the coast of Siberia, debris from
the ship was washed ashore on the south-west coast of
Greenland, thus providing convincing evidence for DeLong's
theory that, providing a ship was strong enough to withstand
pressure from the ice, it might be possible to drift to the
North Pole with the ice floes. Nansen decided to make an
attempt himself even though he estimated that the resulting
voyage might last three years. King Oscar II of Norway was an
enthusiastic supporter and donated money to Nansen's
expedition.[70] Lieutenant Hjalmar Johansen described their
Christmas festivities:

---

[69] He is referring to the brave endeavours of Stanley in finding Livingstone and
also to the tragic death of George W. DeLong and his men in the Lena Delta.

[70] Roald Amundsen, later to lead the first party to the South Pole, asked if he
could join the expedition, but Nansen felt that he was too young.

Our first Christmas in the Arctic regions was upon us, and the saloon of the Fram *resounded with the old greeting of "A Merry Christmas!" We kept Christmas all by ourselves, free and independent of everybody, in our own ice-bound kingdom. We did not need to trouble ourselves about authority and laws; we had none other than those we ourselves made; and our little community thrived admirably. Yet how much should we have liked to be among the dear ones at home, if only for a little while! Thoughts every now and then overcame us like a warm current, thawing all the ice which separated us from the south, and then everything up there in the darkness and the cold became quite light and warm.*

We were seated round the table on Christmas Eve, in our thick woollen jerseys or anoraks, when suddenly an elegantly dressed person, with collar and cuffs and a white tie, stood in our midst. It was Scott-Hansen, who had dressed in his cabin for the occasion. He looked just as if he had come straight from Norway with greetings as he shook hands with us all. From the captain's cabin came another well-dressed figure. This was our commander, who, in his usual quiet way, silently took his seat. All this seemed to us like a breath of civilization.

After supper Nansen fetched two boxes from his cabin. They contained presents to us all from Scott-Nansen's mother and fiancée. *With child-like pleasure we received our gifts of knives, pipes, cigarettes, etc. I got a target with darts, and I think it would have pleased the fair donors if they could have seen how, on many an evening and far into the night, we amused ourselves with this game, winning cigarettes and gingerbread from each other as a result of our skill.*

Cakes, which did great honour to Juell, almonds and raisins and other fruit, as well as some toddy, were then placed on the table. The organ was out of order, and Mogstad had not yet got out his fiddle, so I had to play on my accordion.[71] *And then we sang, and Nansen gave us some recititations. Now and then we took a trip on deck, and it was then that the absolute solitariness of our position impressed itself upon us, with the magnificent moonlight shining over the endless ice-fields around us which separated us from civilization. It was very cold, the temperature being 36° below zero.*

~1894~

As the youngest child of the 9th Earl of Southesk, the Hon. David Wynford Carnegie was expected to make his own way in the world – but took time to find his feet. After his parents had taken him away from Charterhouse, in favour of private tutors, he failed to complete the course at the Royal Indian Engineering College, before moving on to a tea plantation in Ceylon. Finding this rather dull, he sailed for Australia, with his friend, Lord Percy Douglas.[72] Having arrived at Albany, Western Australia, in September 1892, the pair immediately caught a heavy dose of 'gold fever'. However, after just nine months as a prospector, Carnegie had exhausted his meagre resources and was forced to take a job at Bayley's Reward mine in Coolgardie. Lord Percy's appointment as director of a new mining company then permitted Carnegie to resume his prospecting activities. With two fellow prospectors, he spent Christmas some 50 miles from Coolgardie:

---

[71] Lieutenant Sigurd Scott-Hansen, Norwegian Navy, who was responsible for taking the meteorological, astronomical and magnetic observations; Adolf Juell, steward and cook; Ivar Mogstad, general hand.

[72] Lord Percy Douglas (later 10th Marquess of Queensbury), second son of the 9th Marquess of Queensbury and elder brother of Lord Alfred Douglas, Oscar Wilde's ill-fated 'beau'.

Christmas Eve, 1894, saw us in the vicinity of Mount Monger, where a few men were working on an alluvial patch and getting a little gold. A lucky storm had filled a deep clay-hole on the flat running north-west from the hills, and here we were at last enabled to get the camels a cheap drink; for over six weeks we had not seen a drop of fresh water beyond what, with infinite labour, we had condensed, with the one exception of the small rock-hole I found at Cowarna. My entry in my journal for Christmas Day is short and sweet: "Xmas Day, 1894. Wash clothes. Write diary. Plot course." We had no Christmas fare to make our hearts glad, and but for the fortunate arrival of my old friend David Wilson, who gave us a couple of packets of cornflour, would have had a scanty feast indeed.

Even in the remote little mining camp Santa Claus did not forget us, and spread his presents, in the form of a deluge of rain, on all alike. What a pleasant change to get thoroughly wet through!

Their fortunes improved and, in February 1895, they were able to lay claim to a high-quality reef, later sold for a substantial sum. The following year Carnegie led an expedition from Coolgardie, across the Gibson and Great Sandy Deserts, to Halls Creek, a journey of over 1,400 miles that took 149 days. Ever peripatetic, he sold up in Australia and returned to England, then considered a series of expedition options, before settling on an appointment as Assistant Resident of the Middle Niger in the Protectorate of Nigeria in January 1900. On 27 November that year, while in hot pursuit of a fugitive, he was shot in the thigh by a poisoned arrow. The Hon. David Carnegie died 15 minutes later, having packed plenty of adventure into just 29 years.

~ 1894 ~

While there was nothing intrinsically wrong with DeLong and Nansen's theory, drifting with the ice floes in the *Fram* didn't exactly make for challenging exploring, as Hjalmar Johansen recorded:

Christmas Eve came upon us like any other day, lying here as we did far away from the noisy world and all the Christmas fun. It was a quiet Christmas which we thirteen celebrated.[73] We had a kind of cleaning up of the saloon and the cabins. The weather being cloudy and overcast both night and day, we could not take any observations. In the meantime, however, we could safely say that we were a good way north of the eighty-third degree. Perhaps it was as a sort of Christmas present that we had the satisfaction of reaching 83° 24' north latitude, the most northerly point of the world that any human being had ever reached.[74]

Nansen and Blessing[75] were up in the work-room the whole of the day, busy with some mysterious brew. When the bottles came upon the table in the evening it turned out to be nothing less than champagne – "polar champagne 83°" – undoubtedly the most unique in the world. It was made from spirits of wine, cloudberry jam, water and baking-powder, and there was as much as two half-bottles for each of us.

It seemed, however, as if the true festive spirit was wanting,

---

[73] Nansen decided that thirteen was his lucky number, so that was the size of the *Fram*'s crew.

[74] This is located approximately 350 miles from the North Pole.

[75] Henrik Blessing, doctor and botanist.

for this Christmas was not a very lively one. We spoke little, and there often occurred pauses in our conversation, which plainly showed that our thoughts were far away.

And there was nothing wonderful in that. There was nothing strange that we thirteen, on an eve like this, should let our thoughts dwell where we ourselves should like to be. No, no one can find fault with us for being so quiet on board, although we were so comfortably off. In regard to food we were perhaps better off than a good many this Christmas Eve; we were well and warmly housed there in the ice-desert, but we were prisoners. We lay, far away from the world, fast in the frozen sea, where all life was extinct, and in the exploration of which so many lives had been sacrificed. With such surroundings one might well, after a long absence from home, think of those left behind.

This Christmas Day we were also treated to "polar curaçoa," which was really good, and in the evening we danced to Mogstad's fiddle.

~ 1895 ~

On 14 March 1895 Nansen and Johansen left the *Fram* and struck out with three sledges, two kayaks and 28 dogs for the North Pole, eventually reaching 86° 13' 6" North on 7 April. However, encountering 'nothing but ridge after ridge and long stretches of old rubble ice with very deep snow and lanes here and there', they realised they could go no further but, before turning south, 'prepared a little banquet, consisting of lobscouse, dry chocolate, stewed whortle-berries, and whey-drink afterwards'. On 7 August 1895, although they didn't realise it, the pair reached the west coast of Franz Josef Land, off the coast of Siberia, named for the Austro-Hungarian emperor in 1874. A storm then pushed the drift ice against the shore and their kayaks would carry them no further. With no option other than to over-winter at this bleak spot, the celebrations described by Hjalmar Johansen were even more subdued:

Wednesday, December 25th, Christmas Day. – We celebrated Christmas Eve as well as we could. We boiled fish-meal and some maize-meal together with train-oil, and then fried it in the pan. It did not taste as well as we had expected, but the bread fried in the bear's blubber tasted excellent.

This morning we had chocolate and aleuronate bread and blubber – a grand Christmas morning breakfast! In spite of everything, we were doing very well; we are satisfied with what we have got, and enjoy life so much, that there are, perhaps, many who might envy us. We have just had our usual walk up and down the promenade, in weather which we shall long remember, and which we are not likely to experience again another Christmas. When we crept out of our hut and got our heads above ground, the whole of the heavens was ablaze with Northern Lights of every possible colour, which rushed like a whirlwind through the zenith, and then drew towards the northern sky, where they remained for some time; while in the southern sky the moon shone brightly.

It seemed as if the elements had combined to make it as pleasant a Christmas for us as they could.

It wasn't until May 1896 that Nansen and Johansen were able to abandon their winter quarters – built from rocks, ice and hides – and make for Spitzbergen. A month later they met up with member of the British Jackson-Harmsworth Expedition, who were also over-wintering on Franz Josef Land. On 13 August 1896 the pair arrived at Vardø in northern Norway, the very same day that the *Fram* finally broke free from the ice. Interestingly the *Fram* had eventually drifted to a latitude of 85° 57′ North, very close to the 'Farthest North' reached by Nansen and Johansen on their sledging trip. Johansen wrote:

> *And now we are home; but among the eternal ice the solitude reigns greater than ever, for no longer does any vessel lie there to disturb the wild play of the ice, and no longer are human beings trying to penetrate its secrets. Or perhaps the ice-desert was now seething with rage, because a handful of men had bidden defiance to the edict that its territory was forbidden ground, and had penetrated into regions hitherto untrodden by human foot.*

In the capable hands of a number of audacious Norwegian explorers, the *Fram* sailed to more northerly and southerly latitudes than any other vessel.[76] Fridtjof Nansen went on to become one of his country's most distinguished sons: he was one of the founders of neuron theory, served as Ambassador to Great Britain 1906–08, was awarded the Nobel Peace Prize in 1922 for his work as a League of Nations Commissioner and was Rector of the University of St. Andrew's 1925–28. He died on 13 May 1930, aged 69, at Polhøgda, his home at Lysaker, near Oslo.

~ 1896 ~

Under the guise of mapping Western Australia's largely unknown Great Sandy Desert – but more probably so that it might discover promising gold country – Albert Calvert, a London-based mining engineer, sponsored the Calvert

---

[76] The *Fram* – which mean 'Forward' in Norwegian – is now the centrepiece of the Frammuseet on the Bygdøy Peninsula in Oslo Fjord.

Scientific Exploring Expedition. Two surveyor cousins, Larry and Charles Wells, were appointed as leader and second-in-command respectively. A party of five explorers, two Afghan camel drivers and 20 camels set out from Lake Way on 13 June 1896, reaching the Great Sandy Desert four months later. On 11 October, at a place now known as Separation Well, Larry Wells decided to split his party into two: while he continued north to Joanna Spring, mapped by Peter Egerton Warburton in 1873, he sent his cousin and George Jones, the expedition's mineralogist and photographer, off to the north-west to carry out some mapping tasks. The main body never found Joanna Creek, which proved to be some 15 miles east of the position marked on their maps, and arrived, totally exhausted and without water, at the banks of the Fitzroy River on 6 November. Larry Wells wrote in his journal: 'My only anxiety now is for my cousin Charles and Mr. Jones.'

Having sent Aboriginal runners to the Fitzroy Crossing Telegraph Station, in order to spread news of the impending tragedy, Larry Wells left Quanbun Station on 15 November headed south with his two Afghan camel drivers and six of his best camels. After just 30 miles the camels were defeated by the daunting sand ridges and they returned to Quanbun. A second attempt using horses – the first official search expedition – retreated after 40 miles and three days, returning on 27 November. The second official search expedition left Gogo Station on 6 December but, by 27 December, 90 miles from the Fitzroy River and down to their last three gallons of water, it too was forced to turn back.

On 18 November William Rudall, who had just recently returned to Fremantle after surveying on the Pilbara coast, was asked to take another party and approach the area from the west. On 19 December he left Braeside Station, accompanied by Herbert Trotman and by two Aborigines, Cherry and George. The heat soon burned through the soles of their boots and they learned to travel in the early morning and late afternoon. On Christmas Day Rudall was pleased to find 'a fine pool of water at the foot of a small waterfall in a sandstone range'. A 'godsend', he named it Christmas Pool. Members of the party carved their names into the sandstone: the carvings can still be seen today.

Despite spending the next three months following a series of 'leads', Rudall and his party returned empty-handed to Braeside Station on 31 March. Two weeks earlier Larry Wells had set off from Fitzroy Crossing with the third search expedition. Shortly afterwards they discovered a crucial error in the mapping of Joanna Spring and noticed an Aborigine wearing a strip of cloth that strongly resembled that worn by Charles Wells. They learned that two 'whitefellows' had been 'killed by the sun'. However, it took yet another expedition before the bodies of Charles Wells and George Jones were eventually found. On 27 May 1897 Larry Wells wrote in his journal: 'I could then see my cousin's iron-grey beard and we were at last at the scene of their terrible death, with its horrible surroundings.' Although the bodies were lying less than a quarter of a mile from the path taken by the third search expedition, they had died on 21 November 1896 so there was no realistic chance of saving their lives. Rudall's party did not return to the Oakover River until 17 June 1897, having lost all their camels in that inhospitable landscape.

~ 1897 ~

Joshua Slocum was born at Mount Hanley, Annapolis County, Nova Scotia on 20 February 1844 and first ran away to sea at the age of 14. Two years later, following the death of his mother, he left home for good. After serving an apprenticeship, he obtained his first command in 1869 on the Californian coast, sailing out of San Francisco. He spent the next 18 years plying his trade. In 1887 everything suddenly went wrong: before the ship he owned and skippered, the *Aquidneck*, was wrecked on a sandbar, the crew mutinied and he later had to stand trial – but was acquitted – for shooting two men. To cap it all, the way of life he loved was changing, as steam succeeded sail. Fortuitously a friend then offered him an old 37-foot oyster boat, the *Spray*, which Slocum rebuilt, plank by plank, over 13 months. Slocum later wrote: 'I had resolved on a voyage around the world, and as the wind on the morning of April 24, 1895 was fair, at noon I weighed anchor, set sail, and filled away from Boston, where the *Spray* had been moored snugly all winter.' During the next 38 months Slocum sailed around the world in the *Spray*. His third Christmas at sea was spent off the Cape of Good Hope:

On Christmas 1897, I came to the pitch of the cape. On this day the Spray *was trying to stand on her head, and she gave me every reason to believe that she would accomplish the feat before dark. She began very early in the morning to pitch and toss about in a most unusual manner, and I have to record that, while I was at the end of the bowsprit reefing the jib, she ducked me under water three times for a Christmas box. I got wet and did not like it a bit: never in any other sea was I put under more than once in the same short space of time, say three minutes. A large English steamer passing ran up the signal, "Wishing you a Merry Christmas." I think the captain was a humorist; his own ship was throwing her propeller out of the water.*

Having sailed some 46,000 miles, Slocum dropped anchor at Newport, Rhode Island on 27 June 1898. In 1902, after making a modest amount of money from writing and lecturing, he purchased a smallholding at West Tisbury on the island of Martha's Vineyard, off the coast of Massachusetts. However, the lure of the sea proved too strong and, within two years, he had established a routine of sailing the *Spray* down to the West Indies every year. On 14 November 1909, at the age of 65, he embarked on a far grander scheme: to explore the Orinoco and the headwaters of the River Amazon. Neither he nor the *Spray* was ever seen again.

~ 1900 ~

In 1873 Nathalie de Moerder, unwell and pregnant with her fourth child by her husband, General Pavel, travelled to Geneva to give birth and recover her strength in a favourable climate. While in Geneva she heard that her husband had died. Four years later, she was delivered of a second daughter, Isabelle, whose father was Alexandre Trophimowsky, her children's tutor. Isabelle Eberhardt was of undeniably exotic extraction: her father was an Armenian anarchist and former priest, who later converted to Islam, while her mother was of mixed German and Russian origin and Lutheran leanings. Isabelle was registered as illegitimate, which was later to cause her serious emotional and financial problems.

In May 1897 Isabelle accompanied her mother to North Africa, with a view to settling there, and both mother and daughter converted to Islam. That November Isabelle's mother died at Bône and, two years later, her father died in Geneva, whence she had returned in order to be with him. Isabelle spent most of the rest of her short life in Northern

Algeria, where she dressed as a man, took a number of lovers and bravely espoused the cause of those opposing French colonial rule. Her journals were notably introspective and melancholy. Naturally, she fasted for Ramadan, instead of feasting at Christmas:

24 December 1900 – El Oued

I have been feeling ill and weak, have had to cope with the side-effects of fasting, to say nothing of the far more serious matter of my financial problems, yet these Ramadan nights and mornings have quite unexpectedly brought me moments of a quiet and pleasurable serenity that borders on joy.

I see clearly now that the only way to lead a quiet life – which is not to say a happy one, for illness, misery and death exist – is to turn one's back on mankind with the exception of a tiny handful of chosen ones, still making sure one does not depend on them in any way.

Arab society as one finds it in the big cities, unhinged and vitiated as it is by its contact with a foreign world, does not exist down here. As for French civilisation … from what I have been able to glean from the Infantry Lieutenant and especially the doctor, it has certainly gone downhill here.

In January 1901 Isabelle was attacked by a sabre-wielding man in the town of Béhima in Algeria, almost losing an arm in the process. Although this appeared to be an assassination attempt, Isabelle later pleaded – successfully – for her assailant's life to be spared. In Marseilles on 17 October that year she married Slimane Ehnni, an Algerian officer in a French cavalry regiment, from whom she was to be separated for long periods. On 21 October 1904 Slimane rejoined Isabelle at Aïn Sefra, a former French garrison town in the

Saharan Atlas, on the disputed frontier between Morocco and Algeria. The same day the town was devastated by a flash flood: the house collapsed, Slimane survived but Isabelle was drowned. Her latest manuscript, *Sud Oranais*, and her diaries and notebooks were recovered from the wrecked house by her friend Général de brigade (later Maréchal de France) Louis Lyautey.

~ 1900 ~

Baron Eduard von Toll was born in Reval (now Tallinn, capital of Estonia) on 14 March 1858, into an aristocratic but impoverished family of Prussian origin. Between 1884 and 1886 he made his reputation during a successful exploration of the Siberian coast, observing in his report to a meeting of the Academy of Sciences: 'We Russians, taking advantage of our predecessors and our geographical location, are in a better position to explore the archipelago lying to the north of our Novosibirskiye Ostova.' As leader of a second expedition in 1893–94, Baron von Toll excavated the remains of a young mammoth and also established a series of supply depots for Fridtjof Nansen and his *Fram* expedition. In 1898 von Toll was invited by the Academy of Sciences to lead an expedition to locate and explore the Zemlya Sannikova, the landmass that was thought to lie north of Novosibirskiye Ostova.

For the purpose he purchased the barque *Harald Harfager*, renamed the *Zarya*, which was refitted at Larvik, where the *Fram* had been built. After visits at St. Petersburg from the Tsar, the Tsarevich and an impressive selection of Grand Dukes, the *Zarya* set sail on 21 June 1900. On 26 September the *Zarya* anchored at winter quarters, in a sheltered bay between Ostrov Nansena (Nansen Island) and the Siberian mainland. Von Toll described Christmas that first year:

Wednesday, 27. XII/9. I 1901 First Christmas 1900–1901. Happily Christmas is here again! [77]

How did you spend the holiday? Our "Children amongst the Crew" helped to make it extremely festive. Tolstov had made a very pretty tree, a construction of wood and wire, brought from Tromsö for that very purpose, with trunk and branches wrapped in dark-green paper, and the ends of the paper on the branches carefully shaped, so that it looked just a real 'Tannenbaum'.[78] It was decorated with Christmas lights, gold stars and a variety of paper-chains, the work of the crew's two father figures, Yevstifeyev und Rastorguyev. The table, on which the tree shone, was covered with a single, large flag while the walls were decorated with paper flags and smaller, signal flags. At each crewman's place there was a plate laden with seasonal treats: almonds, prunes, figs, sweets, pepper cakes and a pound of chocolate, together with two bottles of rum in a single bowl for all to share. As I entered, the crew, who were smartly drawn up on parade, welcomed me by wishing me "Happy Christmas", before "giving thanks" with one voice. Rastorguyev was wearing a sailor's jacket, on which his medal sparkled, while Foma was formally attired as a sailor. Then commenced the distribution of the presents. In all there were 26 numbered presents, among them a box of cigars, a Nansen game, a model of Nansen and the "Fram" in the ice, as well as a pound of

---

[77] The second date refers to the Gregorian calendar, which was widely used in Russia and Eastern Europe until the early Twentieth Century.

[78] Tannenbaum – the German for 'fir tree', which usually refers to a Christmas tree. *O Tannenbaum* is a well-known German Christmas carol.

tobacco, together with paper and hand-rolling machine. The main present was a squeeze-box harmonica, which was won by shy, little Besborodov. Number 2, the cigars, were won by Kluch, who belongs to the "Adelsklub". Chelesnikov won the Nansen game. In addition there were games of chequers and dominos, mirrors, hairbrushes, and so on. Each man also received a mother-of-pearl drinking cup. Mattiessen, as the oldest officer and 'father figure', was in charge of the distribution, during which everyone chatted merrily by the Christmas tree. The room was warm and dry, since the large oil-fired oven, the largest of the three that Nansen had forwarded onto us, provided us with both light and warmth. After the end of the formal proceedings I addressed a few words to the crew, reminding them of the meaning of this evening of celebration of Christian love, without which no task can succeed. "Only if we provide mutual support for one another, in performing our duties, without allowing self-interest to get in the way, will the task that we have begun reach a successful conclusion. With God's help we have already made good progress in reaching this safe spot at which to celebrate Christmas. With his help we will celebrate next Christmas at our ultimate goal and, if he wishes it, we will be spending the following Christmas at home with our loved ones."

Then I wished them all "Happy Christmas" once more, before returning to the wardroom with the officers and the doctor. Seeberg was on watch so couldn't join us in the mess while Birulja wasn't in the mood and didn't appear.

~ 1901 ~

The following year, as the weather improved, Eduard von Toll despatched sledging parties from the *Zarya* in order to survey the coastline and local islands. One of these was led by

Lieutenant Nikolayevich Kolomeytsev, the disruptive commander of the *Zarya*, with whose services Eduard von Toll was only too glad to dispense: Kolomeytsev headed south to establish coal depots for the ice-bound *Zarya*, eventually reaching St. Petersburg, at the third attempt, on 11 November 1900. Meanwhile von Toll's problems mounted, as scurvy was identified in mid-February while other sledging parties achieved little, and returned exhausted.

However, things did eventually improve and, by 24 August 1901, the *Zarya* began drifting with the ice, finally breaking free on 30 August. Two days later they were off the northernmost point of the Eurasian mainland, a place only previously visited by Nordenskiöld in the *Vega*, by the old steamer *Lena* and by Nansen in the *Fram*. On 16 September the *Zarya* anchored off Ostrov Kotel'nyy and, that evening, met up on the island with K. A. Vollosovich, leader of their supporting shore party. By the time essential repairs had been carried out, the *Zarya* was once more trapped in the remorseless grip of the ice and the planned journey to Ostrova Bennetta [79] was no longer practicable. The death from unexplained causes of the expedition's doctor, Dr. Herman Val'ter, cast a pall over their Christmas celebrations:

Now it is over: today was the last of the three holidays. I have left my trusted "children", the crew, to light the Christmas tree and take their place at the table. In their childish way, with unabashed demonstrations of sorrow and love, they have taken care of our dead; like children they weren't allowed to go too

---

[79] Bennett Island, named for James Gordon Bennett, Jr., who had financed George W. DeLong's expedition in 1879–81. It is the largest island of the DeLong group in the northern part of the East Siberian Sea.

close to the lighted tree in their delight. Last year's tree had been put up again, newly decorated by Tolstov, and covered with wax candles.

For the crew's Christmas table – we didn't have separate tables – which was really nothing to speak of, I retrieved everything from the games cupboard, including two sets of dominos and the travel chess game. In a large tin box there were caramels and sweets of different kinds, handsoaps, eau de cologne and many other things. Mattiessen also had a selection of useful things, such as woollen sleeping hats, gloves, jackets and that sort of thing. I was keen to add to the collection from my own things but, not being able to think of anything other than a box of 100 cigars, I consulted Mattiessen, who suggested that I should donate a double-barrelled shotgun as the top prize in the draw. The whole crew, including Jegor, Nikolai and Basilei, were lined up by the tree in the wardroom, all wearing clean uniforms. The top prize, the gun, went to Scherwinski, which gave me particular pleasure, since it would serve as a reminder of our beloved hunter, the doctor, the preparation of whose coffin and grave he had undertaken as his duty during the previous two days.

This greatly pleased the crew, and I also gave fulsome thanks to Mattiessen, who had organised everything so well. For Ogrin I had a special present, a Latvian book that would remind him of home, and also a photograph of the doctor.

The following spring was again taken up with a series of sledging expeditions, as various groups explored to the north. The culmination was to be a trip to Ostrova Bennetta, led by Baron von Toll himself. Before his departure on 5 June 1902, he made a note in his journal (addressed to his wife): 'Today is Mattiessen's birthday. I will give him the instructions, a copy of which I have already placed in the Captain's folder. There is no time to write things down here, so I will also give him, in a sealed envelope, his formal appointment as my successor. I have sealed a letter for you today. Good night.' By December 1902 the surviving expedition members had returned to St. Petersburg, leaving their erstwhile leader to his own devices, as he had instructed. On 22 January 1903 one of the *Zarya*'s officers, Lieutenant Aleksandr Kolchak, was tasked with leading a rescue mission.[80]

On 18 August the party reached Ostrova Bennetta by whaleboat and found three notes buried in a cairn and a fourth in the fireplace of a ruined hut. In words eerily reminiscent of those left by the Franklin Expedition, the latter informed the reader that the party started the trip south on 26 October 1902. No further trace of them was ever found. On 9 September 1900 von Toll wrote in his journal: 'Here I have given my instructions to bury the box with 48 canisters of preserved *shchi* [cabbage soup], soldered canisters with 6 kg of dried bread, a soldered canister with 6 kg of oatmeal, soldered canister containing about 1.6 kg of sugar, 4 kg of chocolate, 7 plates and one brick of tea. This hole is marked by a wooden cross.' In 1973 one of von Toll's food depots, buried five feet underground, was rediscovered by Russian scientists and, according to Dmitry Shparo, 'the canned soup with meat proved to be very tasty'. Further samples were tested in August 2004 and pronounced to be perfectly safe to eat. It is proposed that controlled experiments will continue to be carried out on these provisions until the year 2050.

---

[80] Admiral Aleksandr Kolchak was commander of the Russian Black Sea Fleet 1916–17 and was later an important leader of White Russian forces in their struggle against the Bolsheviks (literally 'majority'). He was executed by the Bolsheviks on 7 February 1920.

~ 1902 ~

Annie Royle Taylor was born at Egremont in Cheshire in 1856. Sickly as a child, she later recovered her health and, with it, a strong Christian faith. Contrary to her father's wishes, she received some medical training in London, before embarking for China in 1884, under the auspices of the China Inland Mission. She spent the next three years in China, before arriving at the Tibetan monastery at Kumbum in July 1887. In the process Annie Taylor acquired a great fondness for the people and their culture.

Three years later, after spending time in Australia with her father and undergoing a 'cure' at Darjeeling, she tried to return to Tibet but, harassed by the authorities, sought refuge in the monastery at Tumlong in Sikkim. While there she met Pontso, a 19-year-old Tibetan from Lhasa, who was to become her faithful servant during the years to come. She learned to speak Tibetan and, after spending some time with Pontso, her first convert, in Calcutta, returned to China, determined to visit 'the forbidden land'. On 2 September 1892 her party of six set off from Tau-Chau in China, eventually crossing Tibet to Ta-Chien-Lu, the south-eastern gateway into the country. The journey of over 1,200 miles took seven months and ten days. That Christmas Taylor wrote in her diary:

December 20 – I made two puddings of some suet that I begged, a few currents, some black sugar, and a little flour. One is to be for Christmas Day. The cold is extreme, and sitting all day is much more trying than riding this weather. We tried to get the chief to come with us, but up to evening it was not decided. We exchanged some cotton for cheese. It is done up in skins, and is very good. We also exchanged a little cotton-wool for butter.

December 25 – We are resting in our pleasant hiding-place. A nice Christmas Day, the sun shining brightly. I had fellowship in spirit with friends all over the world. Quite safe here with Jesus. Penting and Pontso had to go a long way with the horses before a spring could be found, and so I got tea ready for them and put the pudding on. They were very pleased; but, although the pudding boiled for two hours, it was not warm in the middle. This is a strange climate. We drink our tea at boiling-point, ladling it out of the pan with our wooden bowls, and find it not at all too hot. If we do not drink it at once, it gets covered with ice. We are very, very cold at night and in the early morning.

During the journey the party was attacked by brigands, losing most of their provisions, together with a number of their horses. As well as Pontso, there were three Chinese in the group: one died, another deserted, while the third, the guide Noga, stole most of what the brigands had left behind, tried to kill Miss Taylor and finally betrayed her presence to the Tibetan authorities. Annie Royle Taylor eventually resigned from the China Inland Mission and established her own organisation, the short-lived Tibetan Pioneer Mission. For some years she lived at Yatung, on the frontier with Sikkim, before returning to England in 1907.

~ 1902 ~

Sir Clements Markham,[81] a veteran of the 1850–51 search for Sir John Franklin, as a midshipman in HMS *Assistance*, was the

---

[81] Exploration could be an incestuous business: the biography of Sir Clements Markham KCB FRS, was written by his cousin, Admiral Sir Albert Markham KCB, who had achieved the then 'Farthest North' in 1876.

inspiration behind the British Antarctic Expedition 1901–04. Seven years earlier, as President of the Royal Geographical Society, he had invited the Royal Society to help fund an expedition. Five years elapsed before he reached the point where the government offered to match the funds he had raised, by contributing £45,000. The expedition leader was Commander Robert Falcon Scott RN. Their ship, the *Discovery*, was built in Dundee to the expedition's specifications: innovative wooden construction to withstand the pressure of the ice; a reinforced bow to force her way through it; auxiliary engines; and exceptional storage space for a voyage that was to last 33 months, including two years stuck in the pack ice.[82] The *Discovery* reached Antarctica – via New Zealand – on 8 January 1902. On 2 November that year Scott led the southward venture that formed the centrepiece of his expedition. Christmas Day found Scott and his two companions – Merchant Navy officer Ernest 'Nemo' Shackleton and assistant surgeon and talented artist Edward Wilson – in good spirits. Scott wrote:

For a week we have looked forward to this day with childish delight ... When we awoke to wish each other 'A merry Christmas' the sun was shining warmly through our green canvas roof. We were outside in a twinkling, to find the sky gloriously clear and bright, with not a single cloud in its vast arch. Away to the westward stretched the long line of gleaming coastline; the sunlight danced and sparkled in the snow beneath our feet, and not a breath of wind disturbed the serenity of the scene ... Then breakfast was ready, and before each of us

---

[82] The *Discovery* returned from her mooring on the River Thames to her home city in 1986.

*lay a whole pannikin-full of biscuit and seal-liver, fried in
bacon and pemmican fat.*

After walking almost 11 miles that day, the group had a
'Christmas wash and brush-up' before tackling their Christmas
hoosh,[83] with a double 'whack' of everything. Scott continued:

*Meanwhile I had observed Shackleton ferreting about in his
bundle, out of which he presently produced a spare sock, and
stowed away in the toe of that sock was a small round object
about the size of a cricket ball, which when brought to light,
proved to be a noble 'plum-pudding'. Another dive into his
lucky-bag and out came a crumpled piece of artificial holly.
Heated in the cocoa, our plum-pudding was soon steaming hot,
and stood on the cooker-lid crowned with its decoration.*

On 30 December they made camp before Scott, ordering
Shackleton to stay behind with the dogs, walked a further two
miles south with Wilson, reaching 82° 17′ South, 300 miles
further south than any previous attempt and just 480 miles
from the South Pole. They turned round the following day
and Shackleton never forgave Scott for cutting him out of the
'Farthest South' attempt. On 3 February 1903 the party
returned to the *Discovery*, having covered 960 miles in 93 days.
The following summer the expedition focused on its scientific
objectives and there was no second attempt to reach the
South Pole. On 16 February 1904 the *Discovery* finally broke
free from the grip of the ice, but only with the help of
explosives, and the expedition returned to Portsmouth, via

[83] A corruption of a North American Indian word 'hooch' (drink), adapted by
Polar explorers for any food that can be consumed in liquid form.

New Zealand, on 10 September 1904. In an undated letter, written after his return to England, Scott wrote to John (later Sir John) Keltie, Secretary of the Royal Geographical Society, that 'Shackleton's dismissal is final & his appointment will not be reconsidered whatever happens'.[84] There was to be no reconciliation between these two great explorers.

~ 1902 ~

Dr. Otto Nordenskjöld, a geologist and nephew of Adolf Nordenskiöld, led the Swedish Antarctic Expedition 1901–04. On 16 October 1901 he and his team of seven scientists left Gothenburg in the *Antarctica*. On 9 February 1902 the scientists were dropped off at their 'wintering-station' at Snow Hill, near Seymour Island, where they expected to spend the next 12 months. Meanwhile, the *Antarctica* returned to the Falkland Islands. That Christmas the scientists' morale was still high, as Nordenskjöld described:

The days sped on rapidly towards Christmas, the great feast of the year. Christmas Eve was a fine sunshiny day, but it was not before late in the afternoon that arrangements were made calculated to call forth feelings peculiar to the festival. The table was decorated with flags, and a bouquet was formed of the best materials the station afforded – chosen stalks of shoe-hay, and the withered remains of a Christmas nosegay I had received a year before. Supper consisted, according to the good old Swedish custom, of stock-fish, porridge and mince-pies. When the phonograph was taken out and played the old Yule hymn, "All hail, thou Morning Star so fair!" I fancy everyone dreamed

[84] Royal Geographical Society ref. RFS 4a.

*himself far away across the sea, though none expressed his
thoughts in words.*

Meanwhile Dr. Gunnar Andersson, a geologist who had
joined the expedition at the Falkland Islands and now
assumed command, was unsuccessfully trying to reach Snow
Hill in the *Antarctica*:

*We lay here fast in the ice over Christmas – a Yule spent amid
dazzling sunshine, but darkened by gloomy apprehensions.
Day after day the same cloudless, calm, sunny weather
prevailed – weather so clear that from the crow's nest we could
see Cockburn Island far away to the south. The distance was so
great that the precipitous shore lay hidden below the horizon,
but the plateau and the conical peak were easily
distinguishable. Cockburn Island! That was almost the same
thing as Snow Hill – only twelve miles from the wintering
station. Every time our comrades there looked out of the
windows of their sleeping rooms, or came out of the house, they
could not help but immediately catch sight of this immense sea-
mark at the entrance of the Admiralty Sound or Admiralty
Inlet, as we then called it. When we stood up in the crow's nest
and looked at the little dark speck that rose far away amidst the
world of whiteness, we felt more deeply than ever the bitterness
of our impotence. Ever since the fight with the ice began we had
been hoping for a change, for an opening in the ice, for a path
southwards, that would at least enable us to keep Christmas
together. And now, the goal almost within sight, we lay
imprisoned here, while the days went past, and the sun, whose
nightly course had grown wondrously short, glided past its
meridian, and left us "cabined, cribbed, confined; bound in to
saucy doubts and fears."*

Skottsberg took the fresh green branches of beech which we had brought with us from Tierra del Fuego for the purpose of decorating Nordenskjöld's cabin, and made garlands with them for the lamps in the gun-room as a kind of reminder that it was Yule-tide. On Christmas Eve we all assembled in the gun-room, and Larsen, in a few hearty words, proposed the health of our comrades at Snow Hill. We all sat there a long time together, singing and joking, but, on the whole, it was a sad Christmas.

On 29 December 1902 Gunnar Andersson, Toralf Grunden and Lieutenant S. A. Duse attempted to reach Snow Hill 'by way of the inland ice'. Frustrated by both terrain and weather conditions, the sledge party was forced to over-winter at Hope Bay between 11 March and 28 September 1903. In a now-familiar manner, the *Antarctica* was crushed by the ice and sank on 12 February, obliging the crew to make a desperate 25-mile journey across the ice to Paulet Island, where they over-wintered in their turn. That winter they lost just one man, Ole Christian Wennersgaard. On 12 October 1903 Andersson's sledge party finally reached Snow Hill, from which the enlarged group was rescued by the Argentinian corvette, *Uruguay*, four weeks later. On 11 November 1903 the *Uruguay* gathered in the party from Paulet Island and the surviving members finally arrived at Buenos Aires on 30 November. While the expedition was adjudged a scientific triumph, Otto Nordenskjöld was left deeply in debt as a result. In 1905 he was appointed to the chair of Geography and Ethnography at Gothenburg University and led expeditions to Greenland in 1909 and to Peru and Chile in the 1920s. Nordenskjöld died in Gothenburg on 2 June 1928.

~ 1904 ~

Although Jean-Baptiste Charcot initially followed his father, a distinguished neurologist, into the medical profession, his real interests lay elsewhere. In 1893 Charcot inherited a fortune of 400,000 gold francs from his father and three years later he married Jeanne, a grand-daughter of Victor Hugo. At his own expense he then paid for the construction of a three-masted schooner, the *Français*, with the intention of exploring the Arctic. Hearing that contact had been lost with Otto Nordenskjöld and the *Antarctic*, Charcot wrote to his friend Paul Pléneau: 'Instead of going North, we should go South! In the South we are certain to succeed, for very little exploration has been done ... we have only to get there to achieve something great and fine.'[85] The *Français* duly went south and was frozen in at Wandel (now Booth) Island for six months. With the ice beginning to clear, Charcot was in celebratory mood that Christmas:

> *At midnight, we entered the wardroom, the bell was sounded, the candles lit and the plum-puddings set ablaze. The 'réveillon'[86] was a joyous, juvenile occasion; never, I suspect, had grown men been so amused by such simple pleasures. The gramophone continued to play until four in the morning, at which point Matha, Pléneau, Gourdon and I started on another square meal. None of us will ever forget this 'réveillon'.*

---

[85] Arriving at Buenos Aires on 15 November 1903, Charcot learned that Nordenskjöld and his crew had been rescued: they were later invited on board the *Français* to celebrate their deliverance.

[86] A dinner traditionally held on Christmas Eve or New Year's Eve; from *reveil* – 'waking'.

About five the wind dropped, then a small breeze came up from the south. At seven o'clock I climbed up to the cairn; the moment had come, I gave the order to light the fires and those members of the crew who weren't asleep started to adjust the moorings; they worked merrily, still wearing the paper hats from the crackers! The Christmas tree was triumphantly carried into our home, and I am able to confirm that it is the only tree that exists today in the Antarctic. The national flag fluttered behind it and, in the interests of 'correct form', the 'Pilot Required' flag was raised to the top of the mizzen-mast. No pilot responded to our request, not even a penguin! I think that these animals, in spite of the gramophone sessions, will not be too sorry to see us go.

After striking a rock off Adelaide Island on 15 January 1905, the *Français* took two weeks to reach Port Lockroy, an inlet on Wiencke Island, where temporary repairs were carried out.[87] Limping into Puerto Madryn on the coast of Tierra del Fuego the following month, Jean-Baptiste Charcot then learned that his wife was not only attempting to organise a rescue expedition but had also decided to divorce him for desertion. During the First World War, Charcot was awarded the British

---

[87] As an indication of how times have changed, Port Lockroy is now the most popular stop-off point for cruise ships visiting the Antarctic, receiving some 6,000 visitors during the summer months. That this is not an entirely risk-free occupation was demonstrated when the 246-foot MV *Explorer*, the first ship specifically designed for Arctic and Antarctic tourism, sank on 23 November 2007, after its special double-hull had been holed by an iceberg off King George Island in the Bransfield Strait. All 154 passengers and crew were eventually flown to safety – but only after they had clambered into lifeboats in rough seas and spent a couple of nights in huts belonging to the Chilean Army. The 19-day cruise, entitled *Spirit of Shackleton*, cost US$10,785 per person, excluding international flights, and, slightly misleadingly as it turned out, had very modest 'One Star' ratings for 'Culture Shock' and 'Two Star' ratings for 'Physical Demands'!

Distinguished Service Cross for his period in command of 'Q' ship *Z1* – which he renamed *Meg* in honour of his second wife, Marguerite – on anti-submarine duties.[88] On 16 September 1936 Charcot was lost when his next ship, the *Pourquoi-Pas?*, struck the Hnokki reef off Iceland while on a research trip; only one of the crew of 44 survived.

~ 1908 ~

Dr. James Cyril Dalmahoy Allan served as Medical Officer on Christmas Island – when it was part of the Straits Settlements – between July 1908 and January 1910. On 27 December 1908 he wrote in a letter to a friend:

We have had a perfect scorcher of a Christmas Day! One perspired at every pore, and wished one had twice as many to perspire from – really a parody on a good old-fashioned day. Of course, one did not in the least realise that it was Christmas! ... Since then, the rain has been extraordinary, simply comes roaring down, and one can't make one's voice heard at all. Now it has stopped for a space and I shall go down for a swim, because after the rain the mosquitoes have come out in their thousands ... What do you think we found in the jungle? A coolie who had been lost for six years! He was fat and well, having lived all the time in a beautiful cave; his bed, upon which he slept much, was of soft feathers, and for food, arrowroot, pigeons, and fish served his needs. He has practically never seen a living soul during all that time, and

---

[88] A 'Q' ship was a decoy ship, intended to entice a curious submarine commander to approach to close quarters, before unveiling its guns and destroying the erstwhile predator.

has forgotten how to speak Chinese – just remembers "yes" and "no". As to the reason for the exile, he ran away for some trivial offence after having been on the island two months, thinking he would never be forgiven, and just die out there. I have him in hospital, but he is really quite fit – quite a weird sort of hermit! He is glad to be back again, and smiles amiably when I percuss his chest.

~ 1908 ~

After a challenging fund-raising campaign, supported once again by the Royal Geographical Society, Ernest Shackleton organised and led the British Antarctic Expedition, based on the *Nimrod*, a former Newfoundland sealing vessel. There were two notable innovations: the use of Manchurian ponies instead of dogs and the first time that a car – in this case a 12-15 hp *Arrol-Johnston* – had been taken to the Antarctic. Neither was conspicuously successful. After the expedition's stores had been unloaded, the *Nimrod* sailed to return to New Zealand on 23 February 1908. On 29 October that year a party of four set off for the South Pole. In his journal Ernest Shackleton described their Christmas:

December 25. Christmas Day. There has been from 45° to 48° of frost, drifting snow and a strong biting south wind, and such has been the order of the day's march from 7 A.M. to 6 P.M. up one of the steepest rises we have yet done, crevassed in places. Now, as I write, we are 9500 ft. above sea-level, and our latitude at 6 P.M. was 85° 55' South. We started away after a good breakfast, and soon came to soft snow, through which our worn and torn sledge-runners dragged heavily. All morning we hauled along, and at noon had done 5 miles 250 yards. Sights gave us latitude 85° 51′ South. We had lunch then, and I took a photograph of the camp with the Queen's flag flying and also our tent flags, my companions being in the picture. It was very cold, the temperature being minus 16° Fahr., and the wind went through us. All the afternoon we worked steadily uphill, and we could see at 6 P.M. the new land plainly trending to the south-east. This land is very much glaciated. It is comparatively bare of snow, and there are well-defined glaciers on the side of the range, which seems to end up in the south-east with a large mountain like a keep. We have called it "The Castle." Behind these the mountains have more gentle slopes and are more rounded. They seem to fall away to the south-east, so that, as we are going south, the angle opens and we will soon miss them. When we camped at 6 P.M. the wind was decreasing. It is hard to understand this soft snow with such a persistent wind, and I can only suppose that we have not yet reached the actual plateau level, and that the snow we are travelling over just now is on the slopes, blown down by the south and south-east wind. We had a splendid dinner. First came hoosh, consisting of pony ration boiled up with pemmican and some of our emergency Oxo and biscuit. Then in the cocoa water I boiled our little plum pudding, which a friend of Wild's had given him. This, with a drop of medical brandy, was a luxury which Lucullus himself might have envied; then came cocoa, and lastly cigars and a spoonful of creme de menthe *sent us by a friend in Scotland.*[89] *We are full to-night, and this is the last time we will be for many a long day. After dinner we discussed the situation, and we have decided to still further reduce our food. We have now nearly 500 miles, geographical, to do if we are to get to the Pole and back to the spot where we are at the*

---

[89] The gourmand, Lucullus, once again – see note to 1831.

present moment. We have one month's food, but only three weeks' biscuit, so we are going to make each week's food last ten days. We will have one biscuit in the morning, three at midday, and two at night. It is the only thing to do. To-morrow we will throw away everything except the most absolute necessities. Already we are, as regards clothes, down to the limit, but we must trust to the old sledge-runners and dump the spare ones. One must risk this. We are very far from all the world, and home thoughts have been much with us to-day, thoughts interrupted by pitching forward into a hidden crevasse more than once. Ah, well, we shall see all our own people when the work here is done. Marshall took our temperatures to-night. We are all two degrees sub normal, but as fit as can be. It is a fine open-air life and we are getting south.

On 4 January 1909 Shackleton wrote: 'The end is in sight. We can only go for three more days at the most, for we are weakening rapidly.' Just five days later it was all over: 'Our last day outwards. We have shot our bolt, and the tale is latitude 88° 23′ South, longitude 162° East … We hoisted Her Majesty's flag and the other Union Jack afterwards, and took possession of the plateau in the name of His Majesty … Whatever regrets may be, we have done our best.' That best – the 'Farthest South' record that stood until beaten by Amundsen three years later – was just 97 nautical miles from the South Pole.

~ 1908 ~

Before leaving on his South Pole attempt, Shackleton had written to one of his team members, Professor Edgeworth David: 'If you reach the Magnetic Pole, you will hoist the Union

Jack at the spot, and take possession of it on behalf of the above expedition for the British nation.' With this goal uppermost in their minds, the Northern Party – comprising Professor David, Douglas Mawson and Alistair Mackay – left their base camp on 5 October 1908. Of that Christmas David wrote:

The following day, December 25, was Christmas Day. When I awoke, I noticed a pile of snow on top of the sleeping-bag close to my head. At first, before I was fully awake, I imagined that it was the moisture condensed from Mawson's breath. Then I heard the gentle patter of snow-flakes, and, on turning my head in the direction in which the rustling proceeded, saw that the wind had undermined the skirt of our tent, and was blowing the snow in through the small opening it had made. Accordingly, I slipped out and snowed up the skirt again, trampling the snow down firmly. A plateau wind was now blowing with almost blizzard force.

About two hours later we got up, and after some trouble with the primus lamp on account of the wind, had our breakfast, but as the wind was blowing dead against us, we turned into the sleeping-bag for a short time. It was nearly noon before the wind died down, and we started off with our sledge, still relaying with half loads, the day being now beautifully clear and sunny. At the 1300 ft. level we started our sledge meter again, having lifted it off the ice while we were going up the steep slope. A little further on we were able to put the whole of our load again on to the sledge and so dispense with further relay work. This, too, was a great blessing.

When we arrived at our spot for camping that night we had the satisfaction of finding that we were over 2000 ft. above sea level, and that we had, in addition to the climbing, travelled that day about four miles. The plateau wind had almost gone,

*and once more we revelled in being not only high, but dry.
Having no other kind of Christmas gift to offer, Mawson and
I presented Mackay with some sennegrass for his pipe, his
tobacco having long ago given out. We slept soundly that
Christmas night.*

David described the group's emotions when they reached the
South Magnetic Pole on 16 January 1909:

*It was an intense satisfaction and relief to all of us to feel that
at last after so many days of toil, hardship and danger we had
been able to carry out our leader's instructions, and to fulfil the
wish of Sir James Clark Ross that the South Magnetic Pole
should be actually reached, as he had already in 1831 reached
the North Magnetic Pole. At the same time we were too utterly
weary to be capable of any great amount of exultation.*

Despite the failure to reach the South Pole, Shackleton's
expedition had successfully reconnoitred the Beardmore
Glacier route for Scott's subsequent attempt, was the first to
climb Mount Erebus, the active volcano on Ross Island, and
had reached the South Magnetic Pole. The expedition leader
was knighted by HM King Edward VII on 14 December 1909.

~ 1909 ~

Robert Harley of Brampton Bryan, Herefordshire and his
wife, Freda, were on safari in British East Africa, as he
describes in his journals:[90]

---

[90] *Diary of a Shooting Trip to British East Africa 1909–10.* British East Africa became
the colony of Kenya in 1920. By kind permission of Edward Harley Esq.

A bit further on she shot a hartebeest for Christmas dinners for the men tomorrow. Mrs Corbett shot a reedbuck and later on a pig, and just before we went home Freda got an oribi. Altogether a very successful day; all shot by Freda and Mrs Corbett.

Dec. 25th. Christmas Day, with the African sun pouring into the tent, but with a cool breeze. This is the second Christmas I have spent in Africa, the last one being in 1903. The mails arrived yesterday and we were very disappointed to find that no Christmas mails had arrived for us. Had a letter from Mr. Roosevelt, enclosing photographs of himself and Kermit, the former with a waterbuck and the latter with a leopard. Freda and I had lunch together in our tent and drank their healths at home. Had our Christmas dinner with the Corbetts. There were also there Capt and Mrs Forster, Ross and another settler. In the afternoon a runner arrived from Stinkop with another mail and all our Christmas things. There is a splendid hamper from Lady Ripley and Hal, containing all kinds of good things, in fact every luxury, including champagne, cigars, paté de foie gras and caviare.[91]

~ 1910 ~

In August 1910 Roald Amundsen left Christiana (now Oslo) in the *Fram* but it wasn't until they reached Madeira a month later that he revealed the objective of their expedition: the South Pole.[92] On 8 October 1928 Herbert Ponting, the

[91] Freda Harley was the only daughter of Sir Edward Ripley, 2nd Bt, while Hal (Henry) was her elder brother, who succeeded to the Baronetcy in 1903.

[92] On 6 April 1909 Commander Robert E. Peary, US Navy, together with Matthew Henson, his African-American assistant, and four Inuits, were the first party to reach the North Pole. It was Peary's sixth attempt.

Expedition's photographer, wrote to Arthur Hinks, Secretary of the Royal Geographical Society: 'Captain Scott received Amundsen's telegram when he reached Australia, and the change in the Norwegian's plans was a subject of frequent discussion in the "Terra Nova" during her voyage South. But it was not known that Amundsen had decided to winter at the Bay of Whales, and it was thought by all that he would make his attempt from the Weddell Sea side, and not come into the British field of operations. It was therefore a great surprise to all the members of the expedition when we knew that Amundsen was on the Great Ice Barrier, a few hundred miles from our own Base.'[93] That Christmas the *Fram* was just three weeks from landfall in Antarctica:

The day before Christmas Eve brought rain and a gale from the south west, which was not very cheerful. If we were to keep Christmas with any festivity, fine weather was wanted, otherwise the everlasting rolling would spoil all our attempts. No doubt we should all have got over it if it had fallen to our lot to experience a Christmas Eve with storm, shortened sail, and other delights; worse things had happened before. On the other hand, there was not one of us who would not be the better for a little comfort and relaxation; our life had been monotonous and commonplace enough for a long time. But, as I said, the day before Christmas Eve was not at all promising. The only sign of the approaching holiday was the fact that Lindström, in spite of the rolling, was busy baking Christmas cakes. We suggested that he might just as well give us each our share at once, as it is well known that the cakes are best when they come straight out of the oven, but Lindström would not hear of it. His cakes vanished

[93] Royal Geographical Society ref. RGS/CB9.

for the time being under lock and key, and we had to be content with the smell of them ... Then we took our seats round the table, which groaned beneath Lindström's masterpieces in the culinary art. I slipped behind the curtain of my cabin for an instant, and set the gramophone going. Herold sang us Glade Jul. *The song did not fail of its effect; it was difficult to see in the subdued light, but I fancy that among the band of hardy men that sat round the table there was scarcely one who had not a tear in the corner of his eye. The thoughts of all took the same direction, I am certain — they flew homeward to the old country in the North, and we could wish nothing better than that those we had left behind should be as well off as ourselves ... In the after-cabin a well-furnished coffee-table was set out, on which there was a large assortment of Lindström's Christmas baking, with a mighty kransekake from Hansen's towering in the midst. While we were doing all possible honour to these luxuries, Lindström was busily engaged forward, and when we went back after our coffee we found there a beautiful Christmas-tree in all its glory. The tree was an artificial one, but so perfectly imitated that it might have come straight from the forest ... By ten o'clock in the evening the candles of the Christmas-tree were burnt out, and the festivity was at an end. It had been successful from first to last, and we all had something to live on in our thoughts when our everyday duties again claimed us.*

~ 1910 ~

After a prolonged marketing exercise by the organisers, the British Government was eventually persuaded to provide a grant of £20,000 for the British Antarctic Expedition 1910–13. Since the Hudson's Bay Company wouldn't sell the *Discovery*, Captain Robert Falcon Scott purchased the *Terra Nova* for a down-payment of £5,000, with a further £7,500 promised when funds were available. Apsley Cherry-Garrard was appointed Assistant Zoologist. By the end of the year the *Terra Nova* was forcing its way through the pack ice and Cherry-Garrard wrote:

> *I don't think many at home had a more pleasant Christmas Day than we. It was beautifully calm with the pack all around. At 10 we had church with lots of Christmas hymns, and then decorated the ward-room with all our sledging flags ... The men forrard had their Christmas dinner of fresh mutton at mid-day; there was plenty of penguin for them, but curiously enough they did not think it good enough for a Christmas dinner. The ward-room ate penguin in the evening, and after the toast of 'absent friends' we began to sing, and twice round the table everybody had to contribute a song. Ponting's banjo songs were a great success, also Oates's 'The Vly on the tu-urmuts.' Mears sang "a little song about our Expedition, and many of the members that Southward would go," of his own composition.*

In December 1911, as part of the support team, Cherry-Garrard accompanied Scott and his companions as far as the upper depot on the Beardmore Glacier, before returning to the base camp at Cape Evans. The following March he reached One-Ton Depot, carrying supplies for the returning polar party. Unfortunately Cherry-Garrard and his Russian dog-driver were unable to remain there more than six days, due to their deteriorating health and a lack of dog food. Cherry-Garrard had no way of knowing that, when he turned back, Scott's party were just 60 miles further south. He was to regret that decision for the rest of his life. Cherry-Garrard's conclusion was that:

Polar Exploration is at once the cleanest and most isolated way of having a bad time which has been devised. It is the only form of adventure in which you put on your clothes at Michaelmas and keep them on until Christmas, and, save for a layer of the natural grease of the body, find them as clean as though they were new. It is more lonely than London, more secluded than a monastery and the post comes but once a year ... Taken all in all, I do not believe anybody on earth has a worse time than an Emperor Penguin.

~ 1911 ~

On 10 August 1911 Fridtjof Nansen wrote to John Scott Keltie: 'We shall not hear any more from Amundsen or Scott before they return, I hope with good news, both of them. To me it seems to be of no importance or interest whatever who might happen to reach the Pole first, but I think there will be much interest attached to their observations along the two different routes which they travel. I mean both the nature of the Ice-surface (and land?) and the conditions of the atmosphere will be most interesting.'[94] Nevertheless, as far as the rest of the world was concerned, it was a race.

On 20 October 1911 Roald Amundsen set off for the South Pole with a party of five, taking four sledges, each pulled by a team of 13 dogs. On 17 November the party climbed to the polar plateau where 24 dogs were shot in order to provide enough food for the remainder. On 14 December the Norwegians reached their goal and, having spent three days taking observations, turned for home. Of that Christmas, Amundsen wrote:

---

[94] Royal Geographical Society ref. RGS/CB8.

Christmas Eve was rapidly approaching. For us it could not be particularly festive, but we should have to try to make as much of it as circumstances would permit. We ought, therefore, to reach our depot that evening, so as to keep Christmas with a dish of porridge. The night before Christmas Eve we slaughtered Svartflekken. There was no mourning on this occasion. Svartflekken was one of Hassel's dogs, and had always been a reprobate. I find the following in my diary, written the same evening: 'Slaughtered Svartflekken this evening. He would not do any more, although there was not much wrong with his looks. Bad character. If a man, he would have ended in penal servitude.' He was comparatively fat, and was consumed with evident satisfaction.[95]

Christmas Eve came; the weather was rather changeable – now overcast, now clear – when we set out at 8 P.M. the night before. We had not far to go before reaching our depot. At 12 midnight we arrived there in the most glorious weather, calm and warm. Now we had the whole of Christmas Eve before us, and could enjoy it at our ease. Our depot was at once taken down and divided between the two sledges. All crumbs of biscuit were carefully collected by Wisting, the cook for the day, and put into a bag. This was taken into the tent and vigorously beaten and kneaded; the result was pulverized biscuit. With this product and a sausage of dried milk, Wisting succeeded in making a capital dish of Christmas porridge. I doubt whether anyone at home enjoyed his Christmas dinner so much as we did that morning in the tent. One of Bjaaland's cigars to follow brought a festival spirit over the whole camp.

On 25 January 1912 Amundsen's party reached their base camp, after a journey of 99 days, during which they had

---

[95] Only 11 of the 52 dogs survived.

covered some 1,860 miles. It wasn't until 7 March 1912 that Roald Amundsen reached Tasmania and was able to break his historic news by cable to his brother, Leon. In summarising why he had succeeded, where so many others had failed, he wrote:

I may say that this is the greatest factor – the way in which the expedition is equipped – the way in which every difficulty is foreseen, and precautions taken for meeting or avoiding it. Victory awaits him who has everything in order – luck, people call it. Defeat is certain for him who has neglected to take the necessary precautions in time; this is called bad luck.

On 18 June 1928, while attempting to rescue his friend Umberto Nobile, who had crashed while attempting to reach the North Pole in the airship *Italia*, Roald Amundsen took off from Tromsø in an overloaded seaplane and was never seen again.[96]

~ 1911 ~

After climbing the Beardmore Glacier on 21 December, eight men in Scott's group were left to pull two sledges, with 12 weeks' supply of fuel and food, equating to some 190 pounds per man. Having covered no less than seventeen-and-a-half miles that day, their hard-earned Christmas meal consisted of pony *hoosh*, ground biscuit, a chocolate *hoosh* made from cocoa, sugar, biscuit and raisins thickened with arrowroot, two-and-a-half square inches each of plum-duff, a

---

[96] Umberto Nobile was airlifted to safety five days later in a Swedish Air Force plane.

pannikin of cocoa, four caramels each and four pieces of crystallized ginger.

On 3 January 1912 Scott selected the team to accompany him to the Pole: Dr. Edward 'Uncle Bill' Wilson, Lieutenant Henry 'Birdie' Bowers, Petty Officer Edgar 'Taffy' Evans and Captain Laurence 'Titus' Oates. In that company Scott probably had no nickname although his parents called him 'Con'. On 16 January they were bitterly disappointed to find Amundsen's camp, before reaching the South Pole the next day. Scott wrote:

> *This told us the whole story. The Norwegians have forestalled us and are first at the Pole ... Great God! This is an awful place and terrible enough for us to have laboured to it without the reward of priority. Well it is something to have got here, and the wind may be our friend tomorrow ... Had we lived I should have had a tale to tell of the hardihood, endurance and courage of my companions which would have stirred the heart of every Englishman. These rough notes and our dead bodies must tell the tale ...* [On 29 March 1912 he made his last entry] *It seems a pity, but I do not think that I can write more. For God's sake look after our people.*[97]

~ 1911 ~

Thomas Edward Lawrence, 'Lawrence of Arabia', was born on 16 August 1888, the second of five illegitimate sons of Sir Thomas Robert Tighe Chapman, 7th Bat, who had

---

[97] Some of these words are on Scott's statue, by his widow Kathleen (1915), in Waterloo Place, St. James's, London, opposite that of Rear-Admiral Sir John Franklin.

abandoned his wife, Edith, for their daughters' governess, Sarah Junner. A precocious child, with a passionate interest in archaeology, he was educated at Jesus College, Oxford, and graduated with First Class Honours in History. A demyship at Magdalen College, Oxford then enabled him to work for three years at the archaeological dig at Carchemish, near Jerablus in northern Syria, of which his mentor, D. G. Hogarth, was the first head.[98] On 27 December 1911 Lawrence described an eventful Christmas in a letter to Hogarth, written from Aleppo:

I got a seal at Tell Kar, twelve miles W. of Jerablus: It will go in the bottom row but one? of the case in the place where three were wanted to fill the line: I have all these three now: – one from Spink, one Damascus, one Tell Kar. This last is quite a nice seal, decent size, and cutting. I should describe it as a tervacyclic discoid: the device may be two scorpions: I am most glad the luck gives it you and not the B.M. [British Museum] I bought it on Xmas morning. We (Tagir, Haj Wahid, and I) got to the Sajur that midday. Then the ass of a driver tipped the carriage over the edge of a bridge into a branch of the river, where it settled comfortably on its side, submerged to the upper window, with one horse completely out of sight, one with its leg pinned under the concern, the last dancing on the other two trying to get out. Tagir and I were walking at the time, which was as well: we were thus able to admire it all without concern – the driver frantically heaving up the head of the drowning animal: Haj Wahid groping in

---

[98] David George Hogarth (1862–1927) was Keeper of the Ashmolean Museum in Oxford 1909–27. A demyship is a form of scholarship, peculiar to Magdalen College, Oxford: Oscar Wilde was another recipient.

the body of the carriage for coats and things, spluttering the while between his teeth about the wives and religions of the horses. The red blankets floating away down stream, gave just the right touch of colour.

We spent hours there, in a steady downpour wading after things, and dragging out the carriage. I don't know what we lost: – I miss a terracotta from Jerablus, and some clothes etc – but we got out more than we expected. The things looked like lumps of mud. Tagir stood it very well, only sighing mildly 'Adventures are to the adventurous' when I fished up what had been his pet umbrella. Haj Wahid took a header off a patch of mud; which was unwise with his spare things still under water: he lost his tobacco box then: and when it ended they had not a match or a cigarette between them. Altogether a very novel Christmas. The unkindest cut was when we dragged out our glorious lunch-bag, specially stuffed in honour of the day. We emptied it out on the banks of the river, a horrible brown soup, with muddy lumps of eatables in it. However we were not entirely destitute, with heaps of water to drink and a walnut apiece.

When the First World War broke out, Lawrence volunteered his services. Having fought a notably successful campaign with irregular Arab forces during the war, he spent the first three years of peace arguing tirelessly for Arab independence. Exhausted by these endeavours, he sought to escape unwelcome media attention by spending the next 13 years in the non-commissioned ranks of the British military. T. E. Shaw, as he was then known, died on 19 May 1935, following a motorcycle accident in which he swerved to avoid a collision with two young cyclists.

~ 1912 ~

A veteran of Ernest Shackleton's 'Farthest South' expedition of 1907–09, Australian geologist Douglas Mawson was chosen to lead the Australasian Antarctic Expedition 1911–14, with the goal of exploring King George V Land and Adelie Land, the segment of the continent that lay closest to Australia. Leaving Hobart in the *Aurora* on 2 December 1911, the group established two bases: the Main Base at Cape Denison on Commonwealth Bay, and the Western Base, 1,500 miles away on the ice-shelf at Queen Mary Land. The following Antarctic spring, having survived a series of dreadful blizzards that provided the title for Mawson's later narrative, the exploring parties set off, five from the Main Base and two from the Western Base. The plan was to be back at Main Base by 15 January 1913, to rendezvous there with the *Aurora* and then to sail back to Australia.

On 10 November 1912 Douglas Mawson led the 'Far Eastern Trek' from the Main Base, the group comprising himself, Lieutenant Belgrave Ninnis,[99] Royal Fusiliers, and Dr. Xavier Mertz from Basle in Switzerland, both of whom had care of the Greenland dogs. What followed was one of the most harrowing Polar experiences. On 14 December Lieutenant Ninnis, his sledge and the six fittest dogs fell into a crevasse 300 miles east of Main Base. The only sign of them was a badly injured dog on a ledge 150 feet below. Mawson and Mertz were left with just 10 days' rations, with nothing at all for the dogs. The following day the first dog was killed, in order to feed the rest. Mawson described

[99] Lieutenant Belgrave Edward Sutton Ninnis was the son of Belgrave Ninnis MD, a member of Sir George Nares's Arctic expedition 1875/76.

Christmas in a chapter entitled, in a rather understated way, *Toil and Tribulation*:

> *On December 23 an uphill march commenced which was rendered very heavy by the depth of the soft snow. Pavlova had to be carried on the sledge.*
>
> *Suddenly, gaping crevasses appeared dimly through the falling snow which surrounded us like a blanket. There was nothing to do but camp, though it was only 4.30 A.M., and we had covered but five miles one thousand two hundred and thirty yards.*
>
> *Pavlova was killed and we made a very acceptable soup from her bones. In view of the dark outlook, our ration of food had to be still further cut down. We had no proper sleep, hunger gnawing at us all the time, and the question of food was for ever in our thoughts. Dozing in the fur bags, we dreamed of gorgeous "spreads" and dinner-parties at home. Tramping along through the snow, we racked our brains thinking of how to make the most of the meagre quantity of dogs' meat at hand.*
>
> *The supply of kerosene for the primus stove promised to be ample, for none of it had been lost in the accident. We found that it was worth while spending some time in boiling the dogs' meat thoroughly. Thus a tasty soup was prepared as well as a supply of edible meat in which the muscular tissue and the gristle were reduced to the consistency of a jelly. The paws took longest of all to cook, but, treated to lengthy stewing, they became quite digestible ...*[100]
>
> *We were up at 11 P.M. on December 24, but so much time was absorbed in making a dog-stew for Christmas that it was*

---

[100] It was later discovered that the dogs' livers, like those of Polar bears, contain very high levels of Vitamin A, and can therefore be poisonous to humans.

not until 2.30 A.M. that we got under way. We wished each other happier Christmases in the future, and divided two scraps of biscuit which I had found in my spare kit-bag; relics of better days ...

The tent was raised at 9.30 A.M. after a run of eleven miles one hundred and seventy-six yards. An ounce each of butter was served out from our small stock to give a festive touch to the dog-stew.

In his diary Mawson described the deteriorating condition of his brave companion, Xavier Mertz:

January 7 – At 10 A.M. I get up to dress Xavier and prepare food, but find him in a kind of fit ... I pray to God to help us. I cook some thick cocoa for Xavier and give him beef-tea; he is better after noon, but very low – I have to lift him up to drink.

There was to be no improvement and Mawson described what happened next in his narrative of the expedition:

During the afternoon he had several more fits, then became delirious and talked incoherently until midnight, when he appeared to fall off into a peaceful slumber. So I toggled up the sleeping-bag and retired worn out into my own. After a couple of hours, having felt no movement from my companion, I stretched out an arm and found that he was stiff.

My comrade had been accepted into "the peace that passed all understanding." It was my fervent hope that he had been received where sterling qualities and a high mind reap their due reward. In his life we loved him; he was a man of character, generous and of noble parts.

At that stage Mawson was still 100 miles south-east of Main Base. He fell down a crevasse on 17 January and was only saved from certain disaster because of the harness attached to his stripped-down sledge. Having been fortunate to discover a snow cairn, together with food supplies and a note, on 29 January, he was then greeted with the sight of the *Aurora* sailing away from Cape Denison as he approached Main Base on 8 February. Fortunately six of his companions had been left behind to continue the search. The *Aurora* returned 11 months later to rescue the party of seven and Mawson and his colleagues were back in Australia on 26 February 1914. Despite the tragic loss of life, the Australasian Antarctic Expedition made a series of important scientific discoveries and Mawson was knighted the same year. He was appointed Professor of Geology and Mineralogy at the University of Adelaide in 1921, organised and led the British, Australian and New Zealand Antarctic Research Expedition 1929–31 and, laden with honours, died on 14 October 1958.

~ 1912 ~

Edward Frederick Robert 'Bob' Bage, a civil engineer by training, was a member of Douglas Mawson's Australasian Antarctic Expedition 1911–14, acting as astronomer, assistant magnetician and recorder of tides. Bob Bage, Eric Webb and the expedition's photographer, Frank Hurley, comprised the 'Southern Party'. Their Christmas was very different from that 'enjoyed' by their leader:

For Christmas dinner that night we had to content ourselves with revising the menu for the meal which was to celebrate the two-hundred-mile depot. But now it was all pretty well mapped out, having been matured in its finer details for several days on the march. Hors d'oeuvres, soup, meat, pudding, sweets and wine were all designed, and estimates were out. Would we pick up the depot soon enough to justify an "auspicious occasion"? ...

On the 27th, with a thirty-five mile wind and a good deal of drift, we did not see the two-hundred-and-three mile until we almost ran into it. By three o'clock the great event occurred – the depot was found! We determined to hold the Christmas feast. After a cup of tea and a bit of biscuit, the rest of the lunch ration was put aside.

Webb set up his instrument in the lee of the big mound and commenced a set of observations; I sorted out gear from the depot and rearranged the sledge load; Hurley was busy in the tent concocting all kinds of dishes. As the tableware was limited to three mugs and the Nansen cooker, we had to come in to deal with each course the moment it was ready. Aiming at a really high-class meal, Hurley had started by actually cleaning out the cooker.

The absence of reindeer-hair and other oddments made everything taste quite strange, though the basis was still the same old ration with a few remaining "perks". After the "raisin gliders," soup and a good stiff hoosh, Webb finished his observations while I recorded for him. It is wonderful what sledging does for the appetite. For the first week of the journey, the unaccustomed ration was too much for us; but now when Hurley announced "Pudding!" we were all still ravenous. It was a fine example of ye goode olde English plum-pudding, made from biscuit grated with the Bonsa-saw, fat picked out of the pemmican, raisins and glaxo-and-sugar, all boiled in an old food bag.

This pudding was so filling that we could hardly struggle through a savoury, "Angels on Runners," and cocoa. There was a general recovery when the "wine" was produced, made from stewed raisins and primus alcohol; and "The King" was toasted with much gusto. At the first sip, to say the least, we were disappointed. The rule of "no heel taps" nearly settled us, and quite a long interval and cigars, saved up for the occasion by Webb, were necessary before we could get courage enough to drink to the Other Sledging Parties and Our Supporting Party.

The sun was low in the south when, cigars out and conversation lagging, we finally toggled in for the finest sleep of the whole journey.

The cook, under a doubtful inspiration, broke forth, later on, into a Christmas Carol:

I've dined in many places but never such as these –
It's like the Gates of Heaven when you find you've lost the keys.
I've dined with kings and emperors, perhaps you scarce believe;
And even they do funny things when round comes Christmas Eve.
I've feasted with iguanas on a lonely desert isle;
Once in the shade of a wattle by a maiden's winsome smile.
I've "grubbed" at a threepenny hash-house, I've been at a
  counter-lunch,
Reclined at a slap-up café where only the "swankers" munch.
In short, I've dined from Horn to Cape and up Alaska-way
But the finest, funniest dinner of all was on that Xmas Day.

In August 1914 Bage volunteered for military service and was appointed second-in-command of 3rd Field Company, Australian Engineers. He was killed by Turkish machine-gun fire while marking out a trench line at Lone Pine, Gallipoli on 7 May 1915. Frank Hurley, who died on 17 January 1962, was a war photographer during both World Wars. The last survivor of the expedition, Major Eric Webb DSO MC, died at Caterham, Surrey on 23 January 1984.

~ 1913 ~

On 17 June 1913 the Canadian Arctic Expedition left Victoria, British Columbia, to investigate the unexplored regions between Alaska and the North Pole. Unimpressed with the funding provided by the American Museum of Natural History and the National Geographic Society, expedition leader Vilhjalmur Stefansson approached the Canadian government, which duly adopted the expedition. Although an impressive team of scientists had been put together for the tasks that lay ahead, few of them either had any experience of extreme weather conditions, or had received any survival training. The *Karluk*, a woefully inadequate, 29-year-old whaler bought by Stefansson for the bargain price of US$10,000, first got stuck in pack ice in early August. The *Karluk* was then left with no option but to 'go with the floe'. On 20 September Stefansson left the ship with a small party, ostensibly to 'go on a hunting trip'.[101] The *Karluk* drifted north-west, towards Siberia and, by 12 November, the sun was no longer visible. The expedition's meteorologist, William McKinlay, later described their Christmas festivities:

There seemed to be every prospect of a very white Christmas, and everything else was pushed into the background of our minds as we prepared for celebrating Christmas Day. Williamson and I had prepared a programme of sports which we hoped to carry out on the ice. On Christmas Eve, when the wind moderated to a fresh breeze,

---

[101] Stefansson never returned to the *Karluk*, drifting on the ice-floes, living among the Inuit and exploring the coastline of northern Canada, until returning to civilization in 1918.

we laid out a course for flat and obstacle races, making areas for jumping, shot-putting, and so on. It was impossible to find completely level patches, so our stadium was far short of Olympic standards, but by dinner-time on Christmas Eve we had everything ready. The Christmas spirit was taking hold, and when the Captain produced a bottle of whisky for the boys for'ard, and another for our mess, there were loud cheers. Officially we carried no intoxicating liquor, but we had a case of whisky on board intended as a gift from Stefansson to the Royal North West Mounted Police when we reached Herschel. There were many requests for the tots of the teetotallers – Captain, Malloch and myself. I put mine up to the cut of the cards, and Mate Sandy Anderson won. There was a lot of laughter and joking, and for the first time in ages everyone was really looking forward to the next day.

At 5.30 on Christmas morning, Williamson, Anderson and I got busy decorating the saloon. We dug out the stock of international flags and hung them from the deck above, draping them all round the walls. Then, with ribbon which Hadley had meant for trading with the Eskimos in Banks land, we dressed everything we could in red, white and blue. On a large piece of sail canvas we painted Christmas greetings and suspended it opposite the skipper's end of the table. Behind his chair we draped the Canadian ensign. The result looked really festive and the boys coming in for breakfast were pleasantly surprised.

After breakfast we held our sports. It was bitterly cold, and muffled up as we were, slithering about and crashing on the ice, there was more likelihood of bones than records being broken. But the hazards brought out hidden resources of skill and agility. There were many minor injuries, but nothing serious, and after a rest we assembled in the saloon to eat our Christmas dinner. I had typed copies of the menu, which everyone tucked away carefully afterwards as a souvenir. Here it is:

DCS Karluk
Arctic Ocean
Lat. 72° 3' 43"N.; Long. 172° 48' W.
Christmas Day, 1913

Dinner Menu
'Such a bustle ensued'
Mixed Pickles Sweet Pickles
Oyster Soup
Lobster
Bear Steaks
Ox Tongue
Potatoes Green Peas
Asparagus and Cream Sauce
Mince Pies Plum Pudding
Mixed Nuts
Tea Cake
Strawberries

'God rest you, merry gentlemen'

When we were all seated Captain Bartlett produced another bottle of whisky and passed it round. In his own, Malloch's and my glass, he poured just a drop, whispering to us to follow his example. Then, 'Fellows,' he said, 'I want you to drink one toast. Stand, please.' And as we stood up and held our glasses high, he led us in the toast – 'To the loved ones at home.' It was a solemn moment, and we were all very quiet for a few moments. Our thoughts were thousands of miles away.

It was a splendid meal, and when it was over the Captain produced one of the boxes of 'goodies' presented by the good ladies of Victoria for Christmas and New Year – cake, shortbread, cigars and sweets. After that we were fit for nothing but lying on our bunks for the rest of the day. In the evening we sat around smoking and listening to the gramophone. We felt we ought to be doing something festive, but the euphoria had gone, we had all over-eaten, and one by one we crept off to bed.

On Boxing Day the expedition's fate was sealed:

A loud report was heard, and we ran out to find a crack in the ice running the whole starboard length of the ship, hard against and breaking through the gangway, and stretching fifty yards beyond the bow. This was something we had been dreading, for it meant that in the event of ice pressure taking place in this area, the ship would be right in the middle of a pressure ridge, and would be squeezed as if by a pair of giant nut-crackers.

On 11 January 1914 the *Karluk* finally sank, leaving 23 people to fend for themselves on the ice. On 18 March Captain Robert Bartlett and an Inuit called Kataktovik went for help, reaching Alaska on 28 May. On 7 September 1914 a dozen survivors were rescued from Wrangel Island by the schooner *King and Winge*: three had died and eight were missing. Remains of four were discovered on Herald Island in 1924 but no trace of the other four has ever been discovered.[102] William McKinlay died in Glasgow on 9 May 1983, at the age of 94.

~ 1913 ~

Travelling round the world in an attempt to recover from an

---

[102] Bizarrely, a human jaw bone and other relics were advertised on *eBay* in the summer of 1999.

emotional breakdown, the poet Rupert Brooke wrote on Christmas Day from Warapei, New Zealand to Professor Chauncey Wells of the University of California at Berkeley:

I'm sorry to have bothered you. I thought I should be able to get straight on to Tahiti, but my boat from Fiji was late. So I'm condemned to stay in New Zealand for a fortnight. That is why I ran out of money, and wired. But I'm all right now.

New Zealand is a queer place. If you go a walk along the road, and happen to look down at the puddles, you will notice they keep bubbling. Stoop down and put your finger in them and you know why. They're boiling. You turn to examine what looks like a rabbit hole in the wayside. Suddenly a strange rumbling proceeds from it. You stand back frightened. An enormous geyser of steam and boiling water bursts from it, plays a minute or two, and lapses again: to recur at a regular interval of 10 seconds, two minutes, an hour and a half, or whatever it may be. The whole country is built on a thin crust of rock and deposit, over thousands of feet of boiling mud and water. Occasionally one can thrust one's walking stick through. A terrifying place. I expect it will give soon. The people are pleasant, quiet, and affectionate. Very English, in accent clothes mind and everything. The women dress badly in precisely the same way the London suburban woman does. It's rather amusing to see. They're more civilized than the Canadians, and have some good laws.

I had a great time in Samoa and Fiji, wandering about alone among the natives. In both places they seemed to me extraordinarily nice and lovable, and in many ways – in manners, for instance – so much superior to oneself. It makes one inclined to believe in the Christian idea that we've come down since the beginning of the world, not up. They seem (especially the Samoans) curiously nearer the Garden of Eden than we. I want to start, or join, a Polynesian Defence Society. Its work will be principally destructive. It will mostly be occupied with leaving them to themselves, and with poisoning or ruining the swine who want to exploit them. The German and British governments seem to me to be working very decently and disinterestedly, on the whole, and protecting the natives. It's the independent trader or planter, whose only idea is to get in, make as much money as he can, and get out again, who is the evil.

I hurt my foot in walking in Fiji, and must have got some wretched and tropical microbe in it. For it won't heal. I'm going to see a doctor in Wellington about it. So I may turn up in February with a cork leg. Otherwise I'm very well and happy. Best greetings to both, and a Happy New Year!

~ 1915 ~

Sir Ernest Shackleton wrote: 'After the conquest of the South Pole by Amundsen who, by a narrow margin of days only, was in advance of the British Expedition under Scott, there remained but one great main object of Antarctic journeyings – the crossing of the South Polar continent from sea to sea.' Shackleton set about raising funds for the Trans-Antarctica Expedition 1914–17: among the larger contributors, the British Government put up £10,000, the Royal Geographical Society voted the sum of £1,000 while Sir James Key Caird, a Dundee jute magnate, gave no less than £24,000 (a generous donation that would be worth some £1,600,000 today). Out of almost 5,000 people who applied to join the expedition, just 56 were chosen. Having been presented with a Union flag by HM King George V, the *Endurance* sailed from Plymouth on 8 August 1914, just four days after the outbreak of the First World War. Leaving South Georgia on 5 December 1914, the *Endurance* first became ensnared by the ice on 19 January 1915, before being abandoned on 27 October that year. Ernest Shackleton later wrote:

> *The task is to reach land with all the members of the Expedition ... On December 20, after discussing the question with Wild, I informed all hands that I intended to try and make a march to the west to reduce the distance between us and Paulet Island ...December 22 was therefore kept as Christmas Day, and most of our small remaining stock of luxuries was consumed at the Christmas feast. We could not carry it all with us, so for the last time in eight months we had a really good meal – as much as we could eat. Anchovies in oil, baked beans, and jugged hare made a glorious mixture such as we have not dreamed of since our school-days. Everybody was working at high pressure, packing and re-packing sledges and stowing what provisions we were going to take with us in the various sacks and boxes. As I looked round at the eager faces of the men I could not but hope that this time the fates would be kinder to us than in our last attempt to march across the ice to safety.*

Lionel Greenstreet, First Officer of the *Endurance*, wrote of 'everybody finishing up feeling full as a tick'. Twenty-eight men now set about the awesome task of hauling three boats over the ice until they reached the open sea. The dogs pulled the seven sledges. In their soaking state the men's *Burberry-Durox* boots each weighed some seven pounds. In five hours on Christmas Day they covered just half-a-mile. The previous year Greenstreet had written: 'Here endeth another Christmas Day. I wonder how the next one will be spent.' That night he made no mention of Christmas at all. Shackleton wrote simply: 'Curious Christmas. Thoughts of home.'

They drifted on ice floes until 10 April, reaching what they were to call Cape Wild, on Elephant Island, a week later. Shackleton soon realised that their only option was for a small party to take to the sea to seek help for those left behind. After an epic 16-day, 800-mile voyage across the storm-ravaged waters of the South Atlantic in the *James Caird*,[103] followed by an arduous journey across the previously-unexplored interior of the island of South Georgia, he, Frank Worsley and Tom Crean arrived at Stromness Whaling Station on 20 May 1916. There Shackleton met the manager, Mr. Sorrle, and they had the following exchange:

> *"Tell me, when was the war over?" I asked.*
> *"The war is not over," he answered. "Millions are being killed. Europe is mad. The world is mad."*

Those left behind on Elephant Island were finally rescued – after three attempts – on 30 August 1916. On 9 February 1917 the *Aurora* berthed at Wellington, New Zealand but this still allowed time for many of the members of the expedition to go to war. Sir Ernest Shackleton later drew up the human balance sheet:

> *Taking the Expedition as a unit, out of fifty-six men three died in the Antarctic, three were killed in action, and five have been wounded, so that our casualties have been fairly high.*

---

[103] The *James Caird* is preserved at Dulwich College, Sir Ernest Shackleton's alma mater.

The indomitable Sir Ernest Shackleton, having just arrived at South Georgia in the *Quest* to take part in his fourth Antarctic expedition, died there on 5 January 1922. His last words, spoken to his surgeon, Alexander Macklin, were:

You are always wanting me to give up something. What do you want me to give up now?

~ 1920 ~

After leaving Christmas Island in January 1910, Cyril Allan lectured in medicine at Hong Kong's newly-opened university, recruited coolies for the Chinese Labour Corps and was awarded the French *Croix de Guerre* for his services in France and Flanders during the First World War. In October 1919 he returned to Christmas Island as Medical Officer and, on 12 January 1921, as he was about to leave for the last time, wrote:

Unfortunately the presents I ordered from Singapore did not arrive in time to give the kiddies their Christmas Tree on Christmas Day, but as soon as the Islander *arrived this time we had it. Well, this is the last letter from the old spot. I shall miss much that I love about the old place: the early morning rides through the jungle before the sun is up, when the perfume of the wild tobacco hangs heavy on the air; and the moonlight nights out in the* Thistle *in Flying Fish Cove, and much else. But so it was written.*

Allan died in Hong Kong on 8 September 1926, aged 44, and was buried in the cemetery at Happy Valley.

~ 1929 ~

Dr. Lawrence (Larry) McKinley Gould was second-in-command of Commander (later Rear Admiral) Richard Evelyn Byrd's expedition to Antarctica in 1928–30. Richard Byrd had already achieved the first flight over the North Pole in 1926 and then, although already beaten by Charles Lindbergh, flew across the Atlantic in June 1927. For his attempt to be the first to fly over the South Pole, Roald Amundsen now advised Byrd: 'Take a good plane, take plenty of dogs, and only the best men.' John D. Rockefeller, Jr. and Edsel Ford helped to finance an expedition that was to cost over US$1,000,000. From an exploration base at Little America on the Ross Ice Shelf, the group flew in a ski-equipped *Fokker Universal* monoplane named *Virginia* to the foot of the newly discovered – and expensively-named – Rockefeller Mountains. Although the plane was anchored to the ice, a fierce blizzard threatened to tear her from her moorings. At that moment Larry Gould was described 'hanging onto a rope attached to one of the wing tips. He was blown straight out, like a flag'. *Virginia* was eventually dashed to pieces on the ice.

Gould then led a six-man expedition with dog-sledges on an epic 1,500-mile trip to provide ground support and emergency assistance for Byrd's historic flight, which took place in the *Ford* tri-motor *Floyd Bennett* on 29 November 1929.[104] Gould followed the route used by Amundsen 17 years

---

[104] Floyd Bennett was the pilot of the first successful flight over the North Pole on 9 May 1926 and was Byrd's original choice as second-in-command of the South Pole expedition; however, he had sadly died in Quebec on 25 April 1928.

earlier. On Christmas Day they were delighted to locate on Mount Betty, near the Axel Heiberg Glacier, a cairn that had been left by Amundsen. Gould wrote:

> We couldn't help standing at attention, with hats off, in admiring respect for the memory of this remarkable man before we touched a rock of the cairn. It was one of the most exciting moments of the summer when I pried the lid off the tin can in the cairn and took out a bit of paper which had formerly been a page in Amundsen's notebook, and on which he had briefly recorded the discovery of the South Pole.[105]

Byrd described Gould's sledge journey as 'the outstanding personal achievement of the expedition'. Unlike many explorers, Larry Gould enjoyed a long life, served as President of Carleton College in Minnesota and died at Tucson, Arizona, aged 98, on 20 June 1995.

~ 1933 ~

After a 'calamitous' and forcibly curtailed school career at King's School, Canterbury, 18-year-old Patrick Leigh Fermor decided to escape a dissipated life in London's Shepherd Market – as well as seeking material for his writing career – by walking to Constantinople.[106] Having left the Port of London in the Dutch barge, *Stadthouder Willem*, on 9 December 1933,

---

[105] On 26 January 1949 Gould presented the original note to the Norwegian Geographic Society.

[106] With the founding of the Republic of Turkey in 1923, the capital was moved from Constantinople to Ankara. Although Constantinople was renamed Istanbul in 1930, it was still commonly known by its former name.

Patrick Leigh Fermor was walking along on the banks of the
Rhine a fortnight later:

*The river, meanwhile, was narrowing fast and the mountains
were advancing and tilting more steeply until there was barely
space for the road. A huge answering buttress loomed on the
other bank and on its summit, helped by the innkeeper's
explanation, I could just discern the semblance of the Lorelei
who gave the rock its name. The river, after narrowing with
such suddenness, sinks to a great depth here and churns
perilously enough to give colour to the stories of ships and
sailors beckoned to destruction. The siren of a barge unloosed a
long echo; and the road, scanned by brief halts, brought me into
Bingen at dusk.*

*The only customer, I unslung my rucksack in a little
Gasthof. Standing on chairs, the innkeeper's pretty daughters,
who were aged from five to fifteen, were helping their father
decorate a Christmas tree; hanging witch-balls, looping tinsel,
fixing candles to the branches, and crowning the tip with a
wonderful star. They asked me to help and when it was almost
done, their father, a tall, thoughtful-looking man, uncorked a
slim bottle from the Rüdesheim vineyard just over the river. We
drank it together and had nearly finished a second by the time
the last touches to the tree were complete. Then the family
assembled round it and sang. The candles were the only light
and the solemn and charming ceremony was made memorable
by the candle-lit faces of the girls – and by their beautiful and
clear voices. I was rather surprised that they didn't sing* Stille
Nacht: *it had been much in the air the last few days; but it is
a Lutheran hymn and I think this bank of the Rhine was
mostly Catholic. Two of the carols they sang have stuck in my
memory:* O Du Heilige *and* Es ist ein Reis entsprungen:

both were entrancing, and especially the second, which, they told me, was very old. In the end I went to church with them and stayed the night. When all the inhabitants of Bingen were exchanging greetings with each other outside the church in the small hours, a few flakes began falling. Next morning the household embraced each other, shook hands again and wished every one a happy Christmas. The smallest of the daughters gave me a tangerine and a packet of cigarettes wrapped beautifully in tinsel and silver paper. I wished I'd had something to hand her, neatly done up in holly-patterned ribbon – I thought later of my aluminium pencil-case containing a new Venus or Royal Sovereign wound in tissue paper, but too late. The time of gifts.

The Rhine soon takes a sharp turn eastwards, and the walls of the valley recede again. I crossed the river to Rüdesheim, drank a glass of Hock under the famous vineyard and pushed on. The snow lay deep and crisp and even. On the march under the light fall of flakes, I wondered if I had been right to leave Bingen. My kind benefactors had asked me to stay, several times; but they had been expecting relations and, after their hospitality, I felt, in spite of their insistence, that a strange face at their family feast might be too much. So here I was on a sunny Christmas morning, plunging on through a layer of new snow. No vessels were moving on the Rhine, hardly a car passed, nobody was out of doors and, in the little towns, nothing stirred. Everyone was inside. Feeling lonely and beginning to regret my flight, I wondered what my family and my friends were doing, and skinned and ate the tangerine rather pensively. The flung peel, fallen short on the icy margin, became the target for a sudden assembly of Rhine gulls. Watching them swoop, I unpacked and lit one of my Christmas cigarettes, and felt better.

Having walked every step of the way to Constantinople, arriving on 1 January 1935, Leigh Fermor partially retraced his steps and, the following March, assisted pro-Royalist forces in suppressing a Republic uprising in Macedonia. On the outbreak of the Second World War he was commissioned into the Irish Guards but soon transferred to the Intelligence Corps, serving as a liaison officer in Albania and Greece. As a member of the Special Operations Executive, he parachuted into German-occupied Crete and orchestrated the audacious kidnap of Generalmajor Heinrich Kreipe, commander of the German 22nd Infantry Division, on 26 April 1944. This successful operation was later filmed as *Ill Met by Moonlight* (1957) with Dirk Bogarde playing the part of Patrick Leigh Fermor. He lives in Greece and was knighted in February 2004.

~ 1938 ~

Having resigned from a London advertising agency in a fit of pique at being deemed 'too unimportant to be sacked', 18-year-old Eric Newby applied to Gustav Erikson of Mariehamn, Finland, for a position as apprentice in one of his four-masted sailing ships. He was found a berth in *Moshulu*, the largest of the dozen or so square-riggers to take part in what turned out to be the last grain race, battling round Cape Horn laden with grain, on the return passage from Australia to Queenstown (now Cobh) in Ireland. Having left Belfast on 18 October 1938, Christmas was spent in the Indian Ocean, midway between the Cape of Good Hope and Australia:

> *At last it was Saturday, December 24th, Christmas Eve. Christmas Eve was the principal Finnish celebration. It was our free watch in the morning, and now came the opportunity for the*

great "Vask" in the slimy little "Vaskrum"; the joy of putting on clean clothes was worth the discomfort.[107] Even Yonny and Alvar had a "Vask", and some of us whose beards had not been a success shaved. Then we put on our best clothes: clean dungarees, home-knitted jerseys and new woollen caps. Bäckmann even put on a collar and tie. This was too much for the more rugged members of the watch, and a committee was formed to discuss the question. They were very serious about it and decided he was improperly dressed for the time and place. Nevertheless he continued to wear a tie, and presently I put one on myself, with a tennis shirt and flannel trousers with the mud of Devon lanes still on the turn-ups. It was wonderful to wear clothes that followed the contours of the body after so many weeks of damp, ill-fitting garments. In the splendour of our new robes we slept till noon. Then, except for wheel and look-out, work ceased for everyone ...

The Captain made a little speech. Addressing us as "Pojkar" (Boys), he wished us "God Jul" [Merry Christmas] and told us to come aft to his saloon after dinner. When he had finished we tipped our caps to him, mumbled our thanks and made a rush below. Two sheets were produced and spread on the table. We gathered all our lamps and lanterns and hung them round the bulkheads.

The food was brought in from the galley. Great steaming bowls of rice and meat; pastry, sardines, salmon, corned beef, apricots, things we had forgotten. A bottle of Akvavit and the set piece, a huge ginger pudding, its summit wreathed in steam.

There were maddening moments of delay while I took what proved to be a series of unsuccessful photographs. Then we made a dash for the table. From then on there were few sounds other than the smacking of eight pairs of lips and an occasional grunted request to pass a dish. We had been hungry for weeks

---

[107] There weren't so many opportunities to have a good wash!

and now our chance had come. After the traditional Finnish rice-porridge I worked through potato pastry, chopped fish, and methodically round the table to the ginger pudding, which was sublime, the zenith of the evening. Alvar, appointed wine steward, circled the table allowing us half a mug of Akvavit each, and the starboard watch, who had already eaten, came in in bunches to cry "God Jul, Pojkar!"

When the others had given up, Sandell and I were still plugging on steadily. He turned to me, his face distorted by a great piece of pudding, a little rice gleaming in his black beard. "To spik notting and eat, is bettair," he said and carved himself a slice of Dutch cheese. We all loved one another now. Even Sedelquist offered me an old Tatler *containing a photograph of The Duchess in Newmarket boots and raincoat at a very wet point-to-point. "Oh, say you, I think he is fon in bed, yes?" "No." I took a good look at The Duke gazing myopically over her shoulder before I remembered that Sedelquist always got his genders mixed.*

Each of us had been given a green tin of Abdullah cigarettes. Shaped to fit the pocket, they held fifty; on the lid, in large letters, was inscribed "Imperial Preference". There were additional charms: each one contained a coloured picture of a girl in a highly inviting posture, more accessible than The Duchess. After dinner brisk business was done in exchanging one for another, and Sedelquist emerged with the best collection. Although I didn't really like cigarettes I smoked half-a-dozen in rapid succession in order not to miss anything …

When it was my turn to enter the "Great Hall" I felt very serf-like and nervous, but my premonitions were soon dispersed. Inside it was all red plush, banquettes and brass rails, very like the old Café Royal. I almost expected to see Epstein instead of the smiling and youthful-looking Captain seated at the mahogany table, his officers around him. He held out a hat to me, full of pieces of paper.

*The one I took was Number 7. "Number 7 for England's Hope,"
said the Captain, and the Steward who was kneeling on the floor
surrounded by parcels handed me the one with 7 on it. I wished
everyone "God Jul" and backed out of the stateroom in fine feudal
fashion, stepping heavily on the toes of the man behind me, and
dashed eagerly back to the fo'c'sle to open it.*

*Inside the paper wrappings was a fine blue knitted scarf, a
pair of grey mittens and a pair of stout brown socks. When I
picked up the scarf three bits of paper fell out. One of these was
a Christmas card with "Jultiden" in prominent red lettering on
one side and on the other, in ink, "och Gott Nytt År, onskar
Aina Karlsson, Esplanadgarten 8, Mariehamn." On the other
two pieces was the text of St. John, Chapter 20, in Finnish, and
the good wishes of the Missions to Seamen who had sent the
parcel. Right at the bottom was a hand mirror and comb.*

*I thought of Aina Karlsson knitting woollies with loving care
for unknown sailors in sailing ships.*

Weighing anchor in Port Victoria on 11 March 1939, *Moshulu*
arrived at Queenstown on 10 June 1939, thereby winning the
last grain race. Fifteen years later, having shown the
photographs of this epic journey to a publisher friend, Newby
embarked on a new, and highly successful, career as a travel
writer. His books include *A Short Walk in the Hindu Kush, Love
and War in the Apennines* and *Slowly Down the Ganges*. He died
on 20 October 2006.

~ 1938 ~

The principal purpose of the German Antarctic Expedition
1938–39 was to secure a German whaling station in
Antarctica, since the country was short of raw materials and

was already the second-largest purchaser of Norwegian whale oil. The *Schwabenland* sailed from Hamburg on 17 December 1938 and the expedition leader, Alfred Ritscher, described Christmas spent off the Azores:

> *At daybreak the meteorologists began the Christmas Day festivities by launching weather balloons, in spite of wind speeds of 6–7; the signals gradually weakened as the day drew on, which made the meteorologists happy, because the observers naturally became bored with the proceedings and the former might therefore be able to claim a height of 30,000m, thus winning an international prize!*
>
> *In the afternoon Captain Kottas gathered together all available members of the crew in order to decorate the messes. In honour of the festival, the ship had also been given a proper tidy-up and at 17.30 the celebrations began with a festive meal, with each mess hosting their own party due to space problems. There was asparagus and ham, not in modest quantities either, but plenty for even the hungriest crew member, since the catering policy specified that each of the 82 men on board should get the same amount from first day to last. After that we all gathered together at 18.30 for a joint celebration in the common-room.*
>
> *How talented hands had managed to transform this stark room with its four bare walls of iron in such a short time! Those who had not witnessed the preparations must have been astonished by the festive scene with which they were confronted. The middle of the four-cornered room contained tables and benches decorated with fir branches, on the port side stood two brightly-lit Christmas trees, as well as two more tables carrying numerous presents, hidden under white table-cloths, around the four walls were hung the national flags, the expedition's house flag and a selection of signal flags. The electrician and the two*

photographers had prepared additional lighting in the four corners of the room; the ship's band somehow managed to find space in a niche on the starboard side.

Three of the expedition's leaders had generously paid for silver-labelled bottles of Bill-Bräu beer by each place at the table, which lent an inviting effect to the whole. After my short welcoming speech – in which I spoke about the object and goals of our mutual undertaking, the necessity for total commitment from all those involved and the importance of working together as a team, while anticipating a successful conclusion to our mission and wishing everyone a happy Christmas – came the ceremonial distribution of the presents. The ship's band, a fiddle, an accordion, a zither and a flute, had become very accomplished during seven days of rehearsals and their Christmas carols and folk songs were enthusiastically applauded. From the same spot Captain Kraul then delivered, in a most entertaining manner, with both words and actions, well-received tales of derring-do.

As the evening went on and the mood became more infectious, so new talents were tempted into the limelight, notably the vocal soloists, the catapult-operator, Wilhelm Hartmann, and the sailor, Emil Brandt. Their repertoire was seemingly inexhaustible, as was that of the accompanying ship's band. From time to time I noticed that members of the crew would leave the table for a few minutes, to open their presents and read the letters from their families, at the same time wondering how their loved ones were spending Christmas, some 3,500 kilometres away across the ocean. It wasn't until two in the morning that the last partygoer retired to their bunk.

After arriving at Dronning (Queen) Maud Land, which had already been claimed by Norway, on 19 January 1939, the *Schwabenland* launched its two *Dornier Do J Wal* (Whale) twin-engined flying-boats, *Passat* and *Boreas*, on exploratory missions. Over the next few weeks there were 15 flights, during which some 230,000 square miles of territory were covered by the two planes: around one-fifth of the surface area of the Antarctic was captured in 11,000 photographs but, without any indications of latitude or longitude, one photograph looked very much like another! In order to assert Germany's claim to newly-named Neu Schwabenland, three German flags were planted along the coast by shore parties while a further 13, bearing swastikas on five-foot poles, were dropped onto the ice from the planes at 18–25 mile intervals.

Despite speculation from conspiracy theorists, no permanent bases were established and two further expeditions – planned for 1939–40 and 1940–41 – never took place. On his eightieth birthday in 1959 Alfred Ritscher was awarded the Federal Republic of Germany's Großes Verdienstkreuz and the Kirchenpauer medal of the Geographical Society in Hamburg. Both Ritscher Plateau and Ritscher Peak in Queen Dronning Maud Land are named after Alfred Ritscher, who died in Hamburg on 30 March 1963.

~ 1939 ~

Freya Stark was born in Paris on 31 January 1893, to bohemian parents who travelled widely on the Continent, before her father emigrated to a fruit farm in British Columbia and her mother settled at Asolo, one of the hill towns of Veneto in northern Italy. The First World War interrupted her history studies at Bedford College in London and she volunteered as a nurse, serving in England and Italy. After the war she studied Arabic, initially in London and then in the Levant. In 1927 Freya Stark embarked upon her travels in the Middle East, visiting Lebanon and Syria, and then Iraq and Persia, before venturing into the Hadhramaut in the south of the Arabian Peninsula. She first established a literary reputation by writing about her travels for the *Baghdad Times*. On Boxing Day Freya Stark wrote to her mother from Dhala in the Yemen:

We had one of the nicest Christmas days I have ever spent. In the morning I gave each of the servants a stocking filled with all I could find to take to their masters: a bottle of beer, an orange, a cabbage, lumps of sugar, crackers, and some little presents I had with me. We started off (at nine) on a procession of five horses and a foal, and three donkeys running in and out with servants, soldiers, small boys, rugs – we wound up 3,000 feet nearly (we are already 6,000 here) to where the Amir has a mountain fort. I think we saw as great a view as anywhere in the world: mountains and mountains, studded on their lower peaks with little fortress towers, with here and there terraces and cultivated hollows, and ahead of us the great blue wall of Yemen. At this height there are villages; a Jewish one we passed, the Jews with their curly side-locks all grouped on rocks to see us, looking very biblical. We looked rather non-descript except the Count, who with a wide-brimmed hat might just have landed from Biarritz, and Colonel Lake and Stewart who were correct and handsome in kefiahs.

As we reached the centre of the plateau, which is a huge world of its own, we saw the whole male population drawn up with rifles behind their Amir – a sight in the clear sun. Colonel Lake dismounted and inspected them; the long column (about two hundred) wound ahead with drums and dancing, the Amir caracoled about on a young chestnut to show his horsemanship, we all wound up the steep way to a fort like an old painting on the very pinnacle of the hills. Huge sort of cacti grow among the stones like candelabra. The landscape falls away, on a far peak is the tomb of Job. The little fort is built all of stone. At the gate the army halted in two long lines, and we dismounted and went in by the dark stairs and found our servants who had come on to cook our lunch. We stood on the roof and saw all the tents spread out below, and a sentry wrapped in his scarf sleeping on the battlement with his rifle sticking out over the edge, and I visited the harem, two ladies in silver and blue brocade with ropes of pearl and Indian veils.

In the afternoon we walked down by a cleft of a valley, and got home after two hours of this strenuous exercise in the light of evening. We found that the servants at our rest house had decorated our table for Christmas, and we had a plum pudding with flames. We drank to all our beloved and I wondered what you were doing just then. Today, we are slack and pleasantly lazy. The old Amir uncle has come to see Colonel Lake and we have escaped round the corner of the house and are writing in the sun.

During the Second World War, Freya Stark worked for British Intelligence, effectively countering Axis propaganda in the Middle East. Between 1934 and 1976 she wrote 21 books, including four volumes of autobiography. She was created Dame of the British Empire in 1972 and died at Asolo on 9 May 1993.

~ 1968 ~

The first manned mission to the Moon, *Apollo 8*, entered lunar orbit on Christmas Eve 1968. That evening Frank Borman, the Commander; Jim Lovell, the Command Module Pilot; and William Anders, the Lunar Module Pilot, broadcast live on television.[108] Having shown pictures of the Earth and Moon, as seen from *Apollo 8*, Jim Lovell said:

The vast loneliness is awe-inspiring and it makes you realise just what you have back there on Earth.

The broadcast ended with each of the crew reading in turn from the *Book of Genesis*. William Anders said:

For all the people on Earth the crew of Apollo 8 has a message we would like to send you: In the beginning God created the heaven and the earth. And the earth was without form, and void; and darkness was upon the face of the deep. And the Spirit of God moved upon the face of the waters. And God said, Let there be light: and there was light. And God saw the light, that it was good: and God divided the light from the darkness.

Jim Lovell read:

And God called the light Day, and the darkness he called Night. And the evening and the morning were the first day. And God said, Let there be a firmament in the midst of the waters, and let it divide the waters from the waters. And God made the firmament, and divided the waters which were under the firmament from the waters which were above the firmament: and it was so. And God called the firmament Heaven. And the evening and the morning were the second day.

Frank Borman concluded the broadcast with:

---

[108] Jim Lovell later commanded the *Apollo 13* mission: "Houston, we have a problem."

*And God said, Let the waters under the heaven be gathered
together unto one place, and let the dry land appear: and it was so.
And God called the dry land Earth; and the gathering together of
the waters called he Seas: and God saw that it was good. And from
the crew of Apollo 8 we close with good night, good luck, a Merry
Christmas, and God bless all of you – all of you on the good Earth.*

~ 2004 ~

When Ellen MacArthur set off on her record-breaking, non-stop, round-the-world solo voyage, she took with her a padded envelope from her mother marked *Do Not Open Until Dec 25*. MacArthur said: 'Whatever it is, it won't weigh much. Mum knows the rules.' At 10.00 GMT on Christmas Day, with her trimaran, *B&Q*, some 1,200 miles off Cape Leeuwin, the south-western tip of Australia, Ellen MacArthur broadcast:

*Right now, we are in the centre of a storm – the only white
Christmas about this Christmas, is the breaking waves all around
us … The conditions are horrendous, the waves are huge and the
boat is getting physically thrown around. I've had virtually no
sleep, I've been in my oilskins now for 12 hours and I'm just
hoping this front is going to go over without doing too much
damage to the boat or to me. Right now, we're in the front of a
storm, so you can say we're pretty much in the middle of the storm.
It is moving across us but it's actually going to slow in front of us
and we'll end up sailing back into that same storm even if we fall
out of the back of it today. I'm sailing in and out of a pretty angry
front. It doesn't feel like a different day, to be honest, I've not been
to find my Christmas bag at the back of the boat – it is just too
rough. I'm just trying to look after the boat, look after myself, just
keep everything turning until things get a little bit better at the end*

of this storm. I'm hanging in there, I'm very tired, pretty cold now, spending a lot of time outside trimming the sails. It's been a pretty tiring Christmas so far but just looking forward to seeing the light at the end of the tunnel in a few days.

There's a lot of jolting and earlier this morning we did get taken by this one wave that literally just picked us up and threw us ... The boat spun to starboard, she landed almost dead downwind and then span 40–50 degrees. Then everything went quiet as the wave broke over the back of the boat and then as that wave broke on the back it slewed the boat round and we ended up pointing back up the wave, and then we had another wave break right over the front of the boat before we could carry on. That's when we were doing 20–21 knot averages so you can imagine what the inside of the boat was like ... It's just really testing. You've kind of just got to hang in there, really. We're in it now, it's hammering us but we've just got to try and deal with it as best we can. The boat is just unbelievable – she has taken so much hammering. We've got to stay fast in this or we will fall out of the back of this and things could go horribly wrong ...

Dame Ellen MacArthur and *B&Q* crossed the finishing line off Ushant after 71 days, 14 hours, 18 minutes and 33 seconds at sea, shaving 1 day, 8 hours, 35 minutes and 49 seconds off the previous record.[109]

~ 2005 ~

With the goal of raising money for charity, the Ocean Rowing Society and Woodvale organised the Atlantic Rowing Race 2005. Crews of two and four – of both sexes – left La Gomera

---

[109] In 1968–69 it took Robin Knox-Johnston and *Suhaili* 313 days.

in the Canary Islands on 27 November, expecting to reach English Harbour, Antigua some 70 days later. The total distance is around 2,500 nautical miles. James Cracknell, double Olympic gold medallist, and Ben Fogle, the travel writer and presenter, found it harder going than they had imagined. On 30 December James Cracknell spoke to Cassandra Jardine of *The Daily Telegraph*: [110]

Christmas Day was terrible. We were emotional wrecks. Cloud-cover meant the water purifier was scarcely working so we only had two litres of water each per day and we were craving, hallucinating, for water. We tried cooking our dehydrated food in seawater but it was horrible and we kept bursting into tears.

For about 48 hours, we could hardly row because we kept breaking down. But we knew that if we called the safety boat, we would have had to stay on it until it reached Antigua. Since it was 400 miles behind with the slowest boats that would have meant being away from our families for even longer. With that in mind, we drank one of the five-litre bottles of fresh water in our ballast, even though it will mean a time penalty.

By six o'clock we were feeling a little more cheerful, so we opened our presents and called our families. My wife, Bev, had given me a Christmas cake and one of the other crews had given us some Jaffa cakes, which we enjoyed. I had kept some letters to open on Christmas Day, including one from my dad, who told me that my great-grandfather, who was a lieutenant commander at the Battle of Jutland in the First World War, was smiling down on me.

The most useless present was from a friend who sent a water-inflatable penis: we couldn't spare any air to inflate it, but it

[110] *www.telegraph.co.uk.*

made us smile. We put on our Christmas hats and looked at the tinsel but it wasn't a happy day.

~ 2006 ~

With his father shadowing his progress from another yacht, 14-year-old Michael Perham took time out from Chancellor's School in Brookmans Park, Hertfordshire, in order to attempt the youngest solo crossing of the Atlantic. On 18 November 2006 he left Gibraltar in the aptly-named *Cheeky Monkey*, a modified *Tide 28*. It was not all plain sailing; just a week out of Gibraltar they encountered Force 9 gales. By Christmas things were slightly more relaxed, as he noted on his blog:

Dec 24: Wow, it's Christmas Eve and Santa has been seen on my rigging. Dad bought two blow-up Santas in Mindelo, mine is hung in the rigging. We have also been singing carols to each other over the VHF radio.

Dec 25: We started celebrating Christmas Day at midnight on Christmas Eve by cracking open a collision warning flare each. When we put that on top of an orange, it became probably the brightest Christingle the world has ever seen.

On Wednesday 3 January 2007 Michael Perham sailed into English Harbour, Antigua – and the record books. In six weeks he had covered over 3,500 miles.

~ 2007 ~

In the Introduction, the 'professional explorer' was described as a 'dying profession' as long ago as 1929.

Observation suggests that this prediction is far wide of the mark and that those with a sufficient sense of adventure will always find new challenges. In the same way that the Scottish Mountaineering Council 'started a hare' when they allocated numbers to the so-called Monros – mountains in Scotland with a height of over 3,000 feet – which led to 'Monro bagging' among enthusiasts, so there are those who now attempt the 'Three Poles': the North Pole, the South Pole and Mount Everest. To begin with the achievement itself was reward enough, but now the time taken has become of paramount importance. On 28 December 2007 Adrian Hayes, a former British Gurkha and Special Forces officer, reached the South Pole, thus claiming the triumvirate in just over 19 months, in the process slicing five months off the previous record. Just 13 years after the feat was first achieved by South Korean, Young-Ho Keo, Adrian Hayes is only the fifteenth person to wear these particular laurels. Over Christmas he wrote on his online diary, available instantly on the worldwide web:[111]

Whatever our problems, all were forgotten tonight with our Christmas party and dinner, which we decided to have Xmas eve. Freeze dried pasta mixed with double portions tonight of freeze dried turkey, rice, and butter. And for the first time we had a dessert – sorbet![112] Powdered drink mixed with, of course, snow. Some tinsel, balloons, poppers, and a musical

---

[111] www.adrianhayes.com

[112] Nutritional knowledge, food preparation techniques and NASA's experience during the Space Programme have combined together to ensure that today's explorers no longer suffer the deprivations and calorie deficiencies endured by their predecessors.

card given to Hans "Let it snow" made it quite an enjoyable evening. And, yes, we are having a white Christmas ...

Naturally everyone's thoughts turned to home today at some stages, and there were a few calls tonight as will be tomorrow morning. For me it's a bit surreal – we are in such a wilderness, and have been for quite a while now, that the rest of the World seems light years away. However, it's hard being away from your family today and tomorrow, and I, and everyone, miss them greatly.

Thanks to everyone for their supporting messages and Christmas greetings, it's really appreciated. Happy Christmas to everyone from myself, Devon, Hans, Max and Evelyn.

Christmas Day was unfortunately the same as every other day of the 44 so far, less our two rest days – spent on the move. However, with not a single cloud in the sky and only light winds, it was a perfect, albeit cold, day. At this altitude (3000 mtrs) the light does seem to play tricks. The whiteness of the snow, set against the topaz blue sky and twinkling like diamonds, in particular, seemed more striking than normal. And, yes, it was a White Christmas – outside of our clothes/tents/sleds, white and blue are the only two colours we ever see![113]

---

[113] As Hayes and his party drew closer to their destination, a drama was taking place just a few miles away at the Amundsen-Scott South Pole Research Station: two employees of Raytheon Polar Services engaged in a fist fight, apparently over a woman, during which one of them suffered a broken jaw. The injury was considered too serious to be treated on site and both pugilists were evacuated in a United States Air Force

SOURCES

Academy of Pacific Coast History, Publications Volume III, published by the University of California, Berkeley, California, 1913–14

Journal of a Second Voyage for the Discovery of a North-West Passage from the Atlantic to the Pacific performed in the years 1821–22–23 in His Majesty's Ships Fury and Hecla under the orders of Captain William Edward Parry, R.N., F.R.S., and Commander of the Expedition, published in New York in 1824

A Journal of the Voyage at Sea in the Bark Anna Reynolds *from New Haven to San Francisco,* edited by F. J. Teggart, published in 1914

The Passionate Nomad – The Diary of Isabelle Eberhardt, published by Virago in 1987

Narratives of the Wreck of the Whale-ship Essex *of Nantucket which was destroyed by a whale in the Pacific Ocean in the year 1819 told by Owen Chase, First Mate, Thomas Chappel, Second Mate and George Pollard, Captain of the said vessel,* published by the Golden Cockerel Press, London in 1935

The Proceedings of the English Colonie in Virginia since the first beginning from England in the yeare of our Lord 1606, till this present 1612, with all their accidents that befell them in their Journies and Discoveries, published in Oxford in 1612

James Cyril Dalmahoy Allan: A Memoir, privately published by T. and A. Constable in 1927

The South Pole by Roald Amundsen, published by John Murray in 1912

Narrative of the Arctic Land Expedition to the Mouth of the Great Fish River and along the Shores of the Arctic Ocean in the Years 1833, 1834, and 1835 by Captain Back, R.N. Captain of the Expedition, published by Baudry's European Library in 1836

The Quest of the South Magnetic Pole by R. Bage, included in *Home of the Blizzard, etc.*

The Albert Nyanza, Great Basin of the Nile, and Explorations of the Nile Sources by Samuel White Baker, M.A., F.R.G.S., Gold medallist of the Royal Geographical Society, published by Macmillan & Co. in 1866

The Endeavour *Journal of Joseph Banks* – the State Library of New South Wales

First Footsteps in East Africa or, An Exploration of Harar by Richard F. Burton, Bombay Army, published by Longman, Brown, Green and Longmans, London in 1856

Travel and Adventure in Tibet by William Carey, published by Hodder and Stoughton in 1902

Spinifex and Sand, a Narrative of Five Years' Pioneering and Exploration in Western

Australia by The Hon. David W. Carnegie, published by C. Arthur Pearson Limited, London in 1898

Le Français *au Pôle Sud* by Jean-Baptiste Charcot, published in Paris in 1906, translated by the author

The Worst Journey in the World by Apsley Cherry-Garrard, published by Constable & Co. in 1922

Journal of a Second Expedition into the Interior of Africa, from the Bight of Benin to Soccatoo by the late Commander Clapperton of the Royal Navy, published by John Murray, Albemarle Street in 1829

An Account of the English Colony in New South Wales, etc. by David Collins, published in London in 1798

Journal of H.M.S. Enterprise, *on the Expedition in Search of Sir John Franklin's Ships by Behring Strait 1850–55 by Captain Richard Collinson, C.B., R.N., Commander of the Expedition,* edited by his brother, Major-General T. B. Collinson, Royal Engineers, published by Sampson Low, Marston, Searle, & Rivington Limited, London in 1889

A New Voyage Round the World by William Dampier, printed for James Knapton, at the Crown in St Paulís Church-yard in 1697

A Voyage to New Holland, &c. in the Year, 1699 by William Dampier, printed for James Knapton, at the Crown in St. Paulís Church-yard, 1703

Diary of the Voyage of H.M.S. Beagle by Charles Darwin, edited by Nora Barlow, published by Cambridge University Press in 1933

Narrative of Travels and Discoveries in Northern and Central Africa, in the years 1822, 1823, and 1824, etc., by Major Denham, F.R.S., Captain Clapperton, and the late Dr. Oudney, published by John Murray in 1826

The Voyage of the Jeanette: *The Ship and Ice Journals of George W. DeLong, Lieutenant-Commander, U.S.N., and Commander of the Polar Expedition of 1878–1881,* edited by his wife Emma DeLong, published by Kegan Paul, London in 1883

Journey Across the Western Interior of Australia, edited by Charles H. Eden and published in London in 1875

Journals of Expeditions of Discovery into Central Australia and Overland from Adelaide to King George's Sound in the Years 1840–41 by Edward John Eyre, Resident Magistrate, Murray River, published by T. and W. Boone, 29 New Bond Street, London in 1845

A Time of Gifts by Patrick Leigh Fermor, published by John Murray in 1977

A Voyage to Terra Australis; Undertaken for the Purpose of Completing the Discovery of

that Vast Country, etc., by Matthew Flinders, published in London on 18 July 1814, the day before he died

Journey to the Shores of the Polar Sea in 1819–20–21–22 with a Brief Account of the Second Journey in 1825–26–27 by John Franklin, Capt. R.N., F.R.S. and Commander of the Expedition, published by John Murray, Albemarle Street in 1829

The Letters of T. E. Lawrence of Arabia, edited by David Garnett, published by Jonathan Cape in 1938

Australia Twice Traversed: the Romance of Exploration – a Narrative compiled from the Journals of Five Exploring Expeditions, etc. by Ernest Giles, published by Sampson Low & Co. in 1889

Letters from the Cape by Lady Duff Gordon, edited by John Purves, published by Humphrey Milford, London in 1921

Lady Duff Gordon's Letters from Egypt, published by R. Brimley Johnson, London in 1902

Labrador – Its Discovery, Exploration and Development by W. G. Gosling, published by Alston Rivers, London in 1910

Cold: The Record of an Antarctic Sledge Journey by Lawrence McKinley Gould, published by Brewer, Warren & Putnam, New York in 1931

Three Years of Arctic Service – An Account of the Lady Franklin Bay Expedition of 1881–84 and the Attainment of the Farthest North, by Adolphus W. Greely, Lieutenant, U.S. Army Commanding the Expedition, published by Richard Bentley and Son, London in 1886

With Nansen in the North: A Record of the Fram *Expedition in 1893–96* by Hjalmar Johansen, Lieutenant in the Norwegian Army, translated from the Norwegian by H. L. Bræstad, published by Ward, Lock and Co. Ltd. in 1899

Relations de Deux Voyages dans les mers Australes & des Indes, faits en 1771, 1772, 1773 & 1774 par M. de Kerguelen, Commandant les Vaisseaux du Roi le Berrier, la Fortune, le Gros-Ventre, le Rolland, l'Oiseau & la Dauphine, Paris, chez Knapen & Fils, 1782, translated by the author

Records of Captain Clapperton's Last Expedition to Africa by Richard Lander, his faithful attendant and the only surviving member of the expedition, published by Henry Coulborn and Richard Bentley, New Burlington Street, London in 1830

Journal of an Expedition to Explore the Course and Termination of the Niger; with a Narrative of a Voyage down that River to its Termination by Richard and John Lander, published by John Murray in 1833

Journal of an Overland Expedition in Australia from Moreton Bay to Port Essington, a distance of Upwards of 3,000 Miles by Ludwig Leichhardt, published by

T. & W. Boone, 29 New Bond Street in 1847

A Narrative of Travels in Northern Africa in the Years 1818, 19 and 20, accompanied by Geographical Notes of Soudan and of the Course of the Niger, by Captain G. F. Lyon, R.N., published by John Murray in 1821

Home of the Blizzard, being the story of the Australasian Antarctic Expedition, 1911–1914 by Sir Douglas Mawson, published by William Heinemann in 1915

The Life of a Sailor by Admiral of the Fleet Sir William Henry May GCB GCVO, privately printed

Karluk: *The Great Untold Story of Arctic Exploration* by William Laird McKinlay, published by Weidenfeld and Nicolson in 1976

Over the Rim of the World edited by Caroline Moorehead, published by John Murray in 1988

The Last Grain Race by Eric Newby, published by Secker & Warburg in 1956

The Voyage of the Vega round Asia and Europe with a historical review of previous journeys along the north coast of the Old World by A. E. Nordenskjöld, translated by Alexander Leslie, published by Macmillan in 1881

Antarctica or Two Years amongst the Ice of the South Pole by Dr. N. Otto G. Nordenskjöld and Dr. Joh. Gunnar Andersson, published by Hurst and Blackett, London in 1905

Travels in the Interior Districts of Africa, etc. by Mungo Park, published in London in 1799

Narrative of an Expedition to the Shores of the Arctic Sea in 1846 and 1847 by John Rae, Hudson Bay Company's Service, Commander of the Expedition, published by T. & W. Boone, 29 New Bond Street in 1850

Wissenschaftliche und Fliegerische Ergebnisse Der Deutschen Antarktischen Expedition 1938/39 (Scientific and Aerial Results of the German Antarctic Expedition 1938/39) by Alfred Ritscher, published by Koehler & Amelang, Leipzig in 1942

Voyage of Discovery, made under the Orders of the Admiralty, in his Majesty's Ships Isabella and Alexander, for the Purpose of Exploring Baffin's Bay, and Inquiring into the Probability of a North-West Passage by John Ross, K.S., Captain Royal Navy, published by John Murray in 1819

Narrative of a Second Voyage in Search of a North-West Passage and of a Residence in the Arctic Regions during the years 1829, 1830, 1831, 1832, 1833 by Sir John Ross, C.B., K.S.A., K.C.S., Captain in the Royal Navy, published by A. W. Webster, London in 1835

A Voyage of Discovery and Research in the Southern and Antarctic Regions, during the

years 1839–43 by Captain Sir James Clark Ross, R.N., Knt, D.C.L. Oxon, F.R.S., etc., published by John Murray in 1847

The Voyage of the Discovery by Robert F. Scott, published by Smith, Elder & Co., London in 1905

The Heart of the Antarctic – Being the Story of the British Antarctic Expedition 1907–1909 by E. H. Shackleton, C.V.O., published by William Heinemann in 1909

South: The Story of Shackleton's Last Expedition 1914–1917 by Sir Ernest Shackleton, published by William Heinemann in 1919

An Interesting Narrative of the Travels of James Bruce Esq. into Abyssinia to Discover the Source of the Nile, abridged from the original work by Samuel Shaw, Esq., published in London in 1790

Sailing Alone Around the World by Captain Joshua Slocum, published by Sampson Low, Marston & Co. Ltd. in 1900

A Description of New England, etc., by Captain John Smith, published in London in 1616

How I Found Livingstone by H. M. Stanley, published by Sampson Low & Co. in 1872

Incidents of Travel in Central America, Chiapas, and Yucatan by John L. Stephens, published by John Murray in 1841

A Complete Account of the Settlement at Port Jackson by Watkin Tench, published in London in 1793

Diary of Henry Teonge, Chaplain on board His Majesty's Ships Assistance, Bristol and Royal Oak, Anno 1675 to 1679, published by Charles Knight in 1825

Die Russische Polarfahrt der "Sarja" *1900–1902 aus der hinterlassenen Tagebüchern von Baron Eduard von Toll,* published by Georg Reimer, Berlin, in 1909, translated by the author

Journal of the Voyages and Travels by the Rev. Daniel Tyerman and George Bennet, Esq. Deputed from the London Missionary Society to Visit their Various Stations in the South Sea Islands, China, India, &c. between the years 1821 and 1829, compiled from the original documents by James Montgomery, published by Frederick Westley and A. H. Davis, Stationers' Hall Court and Ave Maria Lane in 1831

The Last Journals of David Livingstone in Central Africa from 1865 to his Death, continued by a narrative of his last moments and sufferings obtained from his faithful servants Chuma and Susi by Horace Waller, F.R.G.S., Rector of Twywell, Northampton, published by John Murray in 1874

The Romance of Isabel, Lady Burton, edited by W. H. Wilkins, published in 1897

Field Book No. 2 by William John Wills – State Library of Victoria